I AM DJ MICHELLE

How a 9-Year-Old DJ Became a Global Phenomenon

Michelle Rasul & Saida Rasul,
with Rabiah York
Foreword by Wyclef Jean

Copyright © 2023 by Mishel Rasul and Vagif Rasulov
Excerpt from DMC website used by permission of DMC
Published in 2023 by Blackstone Publishing
Cover and book design by committee

All rights reserved. This book or any portion thereof may not be reproduced or used in any manner whatsoever without the express written permission of the publisher except for the use of brief quotations in a book review.

Printed in the United States of America

First edition: 2023
ISBN 979-8-200-83265-1
Juvenile Nonfiction / Biography & Autobiography / Music

Version 1

Blackstone Publishing
31 Mistletoe Rd.
Ashland, OR 97520

www.BlackstonePublishing.com

PHOTO CREDITS: Michelle at Sole DXB event, title page, photo © by Sole DXB; Michelle and Wyclef Jean at Global Citizen Forum 2022, Ras Al Khaimah, page 1, photo © by Global Citizen Forum; DMC crew, page 5, photo © by DMC World; Baby Michelle with headphones, page 7, photo by © by Orkhan Aslanov; Mix Master Mike, 2007, page 11, photo © by Fabio Venni; A-Trak, page 11, photo © by Paul Irish; Roc Raida, page 11, photo © by BrooklynVegan; Michelle with piano, page 14, photo © by Orkhan Aslanov; Jamiroquai at Coachella, 2018, page 21, photo © by Raph_PH – Coachella18w1-121; DJ Q*Bert, page 40, photo © by DJ Q*Bert; Michelle @ The Beach, Dubai, page 42; photo © by Tyler Energy Agency; DJ Craze, page 46, photo © by DJ Craze; A-Trak, page 47, photo © by A-Trak; X-Ecutioners in New York, 1998, page 48, photo © by Mika Väisänen; X-Ecutioners in the Bronx/NYCX near Roc Raidas home, page 48 © by MikaV; DJ Rob Swift, page 49, photo © by Rob Swift; Michelle at the Global Goals for All event, Expo 2020 Dubai, page 56, photo © by Global Goals for All; Michelle at the Art Maze, Dubai, page 57, photo © by Art Maze; Michelle at City Walk, page 68, photo © by Firuz Mirzazadeh; Michelle at City Walk, page 74–75, photo © by Firuz Mirzazadeh; Tiësto performing at Mayday, 2019, page 77, photo © by Ss279; Michelle at City Walk, page 79, photo © by Firuz Mirzazadeh; Flea, page 83, photo © by Fartijo 100; Bob Sinclar, page 95, photo © by Bahia Noticias; D-Nice, 2005, page 95, photo © by Timothy M. Moore; The Jackson 5 from left to right: Tito, Marlon, Michael, Jackie, and Jermaine Jackson, 1972, page 99, photo © by CBS Television; The Beach Boys on The Ed Sullivan Show performing "I Get Around," page 99, photo © by unknown author; Van Halen, 2008, page 99, photo © by GHOSTRIDER2112 - Flickr; Miley and Billy Ray Cyrus at Kids Inaugural Concert, page 99, photo © by Defenselmagery.mil; Michelle, page 100, photo © by Orkhan Aslanov; Michelle at Junk Kouture World Final at Etihad Arena, Abu Dhabi, page 110, photo © by Junk Kouture®; Michelle, page 113, photo © by Firuz Mirzazadeh; Dj Craze, page 118, photo © by DJ Craze; Michelle with Nikaia and Emi, page 120, photo © by Verena Demircan; Michelle at Sample Music Festival, Dubai World Trade Center, page 132, photo © by Sample Music Festival; Michelle at Sample Music Festival, Dubai World Trade Center, page 133, photo © by Sample Music Festival; Michelle with shoe boxes, Dubai Mall, page 136, photo © by Nike®; Michelle at France's Got Talent, Season 16, page 141, photo © by Maria Etchegoyen/M6; Baby Michelle in a blanket, page 147, photo © by Orkhan Aslanov; Michelle, page 148–149, photo © by Orkhan Aslanov. Uncredited photos courtesy of DMC, BrooklynVegan, and the Rasul family. Used with permission.

CONTENTS

FOREWORD 1

HELLO 2
The 2021 DMC World DJ Championships 4
The Opportunity 5
Fantabulastic! 8
DMC 10

FIRST TIME AT THE TURNTABLES 12
Remix It! 13
What a Year! 20
The Best Teacher 22
Michelle's Faves! 25
Mixing 26
The First Skills Scratch DJs Should Master 28
Mom? Or Momager? 31
Practice and Influences 37
DJ Heroes 46
The Gear behind the Music 52

GOING PRO 60
Road to Fame 64
DJ Michelle Is Playing for You! 68

A DAY IN HER LIFE 80
School Days 86
The Lockdown 95
A Note of Gratidude 97

A FAMILY AFFAIR 98

2021 DMC WORLD PORTABLIST CHAMPIONSHIPS 112

FAME 118
What Next? 142

EPILOGUE 150

FOREWORD

At a very young age, a lot of people called me a prodigy. I never really knew what that meant at the time. I was very young and was simply doing what came naturally to me. Now that I am older and understand, I can spot a prodigy a mile away. One day, a few years ago, while scrolling through my Instagram, I came across a very young DJ mixing my material. DJ Michelle was cutting up like she was one of the Fugees. She was doing what our DJ from the Fugees was doing with her eyes closed. Later, when I got to know her a little more and paid close attention to the content she was posting, I realized she is a prodigy herself. With her talents, she will go down as one of the greatest composers to walk our planet. I look forward to following her on this journey. My personal message to DJ Michelle: You can count on Uncle Wyclef Jean to encourage you along the way. Keep doing what you're doing and keep getting better. You are amazing, and the world will soon know!

—Wyclef Jean

HELLO

Welcome to your supreme guide to all things DJ Michelle! You are embarking on an exciting journey with a girl destined to become a world-famous DJ and the youngest competitor ever in the DMC World DJ Championships. As of this book's publication, she is only eleven years old. Her inspiring life is a testament to passion, talent, family, love, and perseverance—and above all, a celebration of Girl Power with some scratching and a beat.

THE DJ MICHELLE FANBASE...

Some call DJ Michelle a "child prodigy" or a "child turntable celebrity." Some just love her music and like to dance. From toddlers to seniors, from every corner of the globe, DJ Michelle's followers are part of a movement of musical positivity. You'll hear from many of them. She treasures all of them. And if you're reading this book, she treasures you.

INSIDE...

* **You'll join DJ Michelle at home and on the road.**

* **You'll get a backstage pass to her shows.**

* **You'll meet her family and friends.**

* **You'll learn what makes her so great, from her talent to her practice to her gear to her attitude.**

* **You'll also hear from Michelle's heroes, legends such as DJ Q*bert, DJ Craze, Missy Elliott, and many more—who are now her fans!**

So let's get started!

The 2021 DMC World DJ Championships

If you're a DJ on planet Earth and you want a shot at making it big, then you already know all about the DMC World DJ Championships. If anyone in your family is a DJ, chances are that they know about the DMC, too! DMC is short for Disco Mix Club—named by its founder, Tony Prince. Back in the early eighties, Tony was a scrappy radio host on Radio Luxembourg, playing dance hits and B sides from the US. One day, a cassette tape showed up in the mail from a teenager named Alan Coulthard. Tony had no idea who the kid was, but when he listened to the tape, he knew he'd stumbled upon magic. Alan had re-created what American club DJs were doing at the time: stitching those same dance hits and B sides together into a medley, matching up the keys and the beats to create one long nonstop groove. So Tony hired Alan on the spot. (Unlike his boss, Alan eventually lost interest in music and grew up to become a lawyer!) Once Tony played the medley on the radio, his fanbase among professional DJs in Europe skyrocketed.

Within weeks, DJs all over Europe were mailing Tony *their* cassettes. It wasn't long before major labels took notice. Soon Epic Records hired Tony to produce an extended Michael Jackson mix, which allowed him to start his own new radio show: *The Disco Mix Club*. Its overnight success inspired Tony to use the name to launch a remix label—a boutique record company that only sells to professional DJs. And since those same DJs were trying to beat each other out for the most radio play, a competition seemed like the natural next step.

On April 1, 1985, Tony hosted the first DMC World DJ Competitions at the Hippodrome in London. The rest is music history.

DJ Michelle at DMC

The crew behind the 2021 DMC World Championships

The Opportunity

In April of 2021, DJ Michelle entered the DMC World Portablist DJ Championship as its youngest contestant ever. Let's see how old Michelle was when this happened and how she found out about the contest:

"Nine! I just turned nine when I entered. Finding out about the contest was super easy because DJing has been a part of my life since . . . well . . . forever. Plus, my dad is a DJ and we always try to keep up-to-date on the latest news surrounding the DJ and music world. One day, my dad showed me the announcement on the internet—DMC World DJ Championships was going to be online this year. And even though COVID is awful, the fact that the DMC World DJ Championships was going online was a . . . what do you call it, a silver lining? Or I would call it a silver, gold, purple, and pink lining, because that meant that any DJ from anywhere in the world could apply and compete. And the first show on the schedule was the Portablist Championship—it just means that you are competing on a portable turntable."

THERE IS A BRIGHT SIDE TO EVERY DARK CORNER!

5

"Anyhow, there we were looking at my dad's laptop when his eyes got real big. Lollipop big. He asked me if I wanted to enter with him. And I wondered: Will I really battle with my dad? Will I really battle with other experienced DJs from all around the world? It might have scared some people, but not me. I screamed and jumped up and down so many times that my long braids almost whipped me in the face."

BIRTHDAY: March 4, 2012

Fantabulastic!

When Michelle's dad asked her what she thought, Michelle didn't hesitate a second to answer:

"That's a dream come true! The opportunity created just for me! Whoa! That's FANTABULASTIC! Out of this world. Yessss . . . YESSSS . . . *YESSSS*!"

And that's what inspired her the most—her own dreams; her own fantasy. She'd always watched past years' contestants on YouTube, and she fantasized that one day soon she would win the DMC World DJ Championships and become the youngest DMC World Champion ever! Can you imagine? Like DJ Rena . . . He competed as a twelve-year-old boy and won! He actually *won*. And that's what Michelle wanted. Once that possibility became a reality, it blew her mind (and braids, too! 🙂). Every time she watched the previous champions, she would find herself behind her decks afterward, practicing, trying something new or creating her own scratches. Because now, well, now it was her turn! And the thought constantly swirling around in her mind was,

Can I make it to the finals? Can I win?

Dreams do come true! Dream big and opportunity won't keep you waiting!

 DMC is the largest DJ organisation in the world with its headquarters in the UK. Over the decades it has successfully expanded into the youth market with music, magazines and the legendary DMC World DJ Championship with branches in over 30 countries.

 DMC was the world's first DJ mix service and still today provides the DJ world with a monthly membership of the latest remixes / megamixes / two trackers / cut ups and promos.

 DMC published MIXMAG the biggest selling music magazine ever which we developed over 15 years with monthly sales of over 150,000 copies. The magazine became the bible to DJs and dance music fans and was pivotal to the emergence and success of the modern DJ and clubbing scene.

 In addition to maintaining the DMC clothing and merchandise lines, the company has successful music compilation CDs including Back to Mine, (once described by NME magazine as: "Probably the greatest compilation series ever').

 The DMC World DJ Championships was launched in 1985 and has become the world's number one and longest running DJ Competition in the world with an uncountable world-wide fan base and cult following.

 To become a DMC World DJ Champion, DJs around the world use techniques such as scratching and cutting to create their own musical arrangements before a live audience.

 In DMC battles, legends are created. Becoming a DMC National Champion continues to be one of the most sought after titles for DJs worldwide! To then become the WORLD CHAMPION is their biggest dream of all.

DMC Champions on all levels have gone on to form major careers—for instance:

★ DJ Enferno (2003 DMC US Champion) DJ'd for Madonna

★ DJ IQ (Young UK DMC Champion) DJs for Professor Green

Mix Master Mike (2x World Champion) DJ'd for The Beastie Boys

A-Trak (1997 DMC World Champion) DJ'd for Kanye West/Duck Sauce

Roc Raida (1995 DMC World Champion) was the DJ for Busta Rhymes

 DMC maintains the world's premier DJ web site. Most DJs recognise the influence of DMC and all of them saw their careers expanding once the company had featured them on the cover of Mixmag back in the day. It is commonly recognised that top club brands such as Ministry of Sound, Cream, Renaissance and Ibiza club culture were all founded on the focus provided to them through DMC's exposure in Mixmag.

 DMC are now looking forward with great excitement to the new generation of DJs. We have recognised in recent years the need and demand for new technology and the DMC Online DJ Championship allows us to embrace all technology. For the first time, the DMC Online Championship gives every DJ in any country in the world the opportunity to compete in the world's most famous DJ events.

FIRST TIME AT THE TURNTABLES

DJ Michelle is the youngest professional girl DJ in the world, but what's the secret behind her success? Let's look back at where it all began!

Remix It!

In case you're wondering what the word *DJ* even means or where it came from, it is short for "disc jockey." Legend has it that in 1935, celebrity newsman Walter Winchell invented the phrase as an insult. It was his way of saying that the guys who spun phonographs—those scratchy vinyl records—had no talent. They could ride to radio fame on the music alone, while show hosts like *himself* had to make the airwaves interesting. But it wasn't until 1941 that the words *disc jockey* first appeared in print, when *Variety* magazine published an article about "a disc jockey who sings along with his records." Here the term was complimentary, implying skill and hustle. Luckily for DJs after that (and maybe because it happened to be true), the old insult was forgotten and the compliment stuck.

Shall we find out when Michelle first became interested in DJing?

"Gosh, I'm not sure. It feels as though I was born with a turntable in my hands. Okay, maybe not a turntable, but Mom did say that I came into the world literally singing."

While all other newborns were crying as usual babies do, my cry sounded like

"Laaaaaaa. La la. La. La. La. LAAAAAAH!"

"Apparently, Mom wasn't too surprised that I came out singing. My entire family is musical. Mom played the violin. I have grandparents, uncles, and aunties who are musicians, too. Guess you could say I was destined to be an artist. And while I like to play with other instruments, like the bass, turntables are where it's at!"

"And then there's Dad. He's been a professional DJ since the time of the dinosaurs. Oh my gosh, isn't that a funny image? Dinosaurs rocking it out. Like what would happen if dinosaurs danced? Is that why the continents split apart? 😳 Anyhow, my earliest memories are of watching him play while I sat, rocking in my crib."

WOW

HA! HA! HA!

"My dad's been DJing since the time of the dinosaurs!"

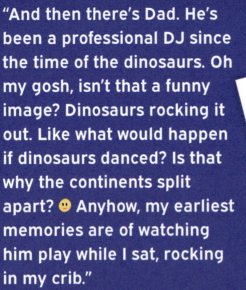

15

Michelle recalls how she couldn't even stand on her own two feet, but there she was, itching to reach out and put her baby fingers all over those shining buttons as she fluttered and flicked the vinyl. There hasn't been a day in her house when music wasn't played. It's in the air, and on the walls—posters and pictures of the greatest of the greats, like Tupac Shakur, Notorious B.I.G., Snoop Dogg, and others.

FUN FACT!

Michelle grew up listening to rap artists more than she listened to regular baby stuff like ABC songs!

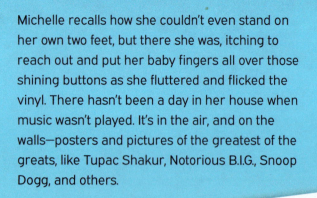

When she was a little older, about a year and a half, and could walk and talk, her dad would lift her onto a big old chair and let her play with his equipment. She recalls these moments with a smile:

"**Holy moly! Oh, how I loved pressing the colorful buttons! I remember pressing one button that turned everything off and I was like,** *Oops, hey! Who turned the music off?*"

Then her dad would press the ON button and she'd reach back out, grabbing all the buttons and handles she could touch. She always felt like she was controlling a rocket ship for music. She was ready to go everywhere and anywhere with all those buttons and levers. And what a racket she made! But her mom and dad were always laughing and smiling and cheering her on.

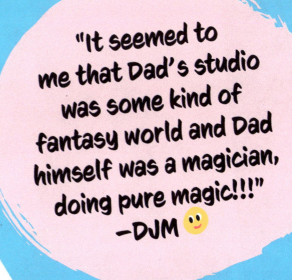

"It seemed to me that Dad's studio was some kind of fantasy world and Dad himself was a magician, doing pure magic!!!"
—DJM 🙂

Sounds like she grew up in a fun home, right? Here is how Michelle describes what it was like the first time she saw her dad play in front of an audience:

"The first time I saw my father performing on a big stage was the year we moved from Baku to Dubai. I was only five then, and Dad was performing for a huge crowd at the Dubai Mall, one of the largest malls in the entire world. It's the size of more than fifty football fields. Ginormous! Right? It even has a zoo and an aquarium built inside the mall. Dad was so awesome that I'm pretty sure even the sharks and rays were dancing." 🙂

Michelle was so shocked when she saw her dad's performance, that after sitting with it a little, she loudly exclaimed her finding:

"Now I know why his name is DJ SHOCK!"

But that's not even the best part. Michelle's dad invited her onto the stage to DJ. To actually perform! Scratching with her dad in front of all those people was the best feeling in the entire world for her. It didn't matter that her scratches were simple. We all have to start somewhere, don't we? And the audience loved it! They were hooting and hollering like they were *all* part of one big family. A musical family. A family with people from all over the world.

FUN FACT!

The Dubai Mall is not only "ginormous" (home to over twelve hundred shops and two hundred restaurants), it is also a free concert venue. Over one hundred million people visit every year, making it a premier hot spot for musicians to build their audiences.

What a Year!

The year Michelle's family moved to Dubai was filled with amazing surprises. Her mom and dad took her to a lot of the local festivals. That was when she first met one of her musical heroes: an amazing artist called Jay Kay, who even shook her hand and signed a vinyl record for her!

"He has a band called Jamiroquai, which is the coolest name in the world. And boy can Jay Kay dance! He glides across the stage as if his feet have wings. I realized that's kind of what it feels like to scratch on the turntables. Like my fingers have tiny little wings. They are little bees buzzing about, itching and twitching, and making magic that's sweet like honey. Guess you could say that my first experience on the turntables was love at first scratch. Love in my fingers. Love in my heart. Love in my family."

DID YOU KNOW:
The members of Jamiroquai have been rock stars for over thirty years—selling over twenty-six million albums and selling out stadiums and arenas around the world. Jay Kay is not only a talented dancer, he is worth an estimated sixty million dollars and collects high-end sports cars.

The Best Teacher

Gosh, Michelle makes DJing sound easy and fun! Does it make your fingers itchy and twitchy, too, like you want to try while reading this? Give it a shot! But it's not as easy as it looks—and it wasn't always easy for Michelle either. At least,

"not when you're first learning,"

admits Michelle. But her parents have always been there every step of the way. Whenever she is frustrated, her mom tells her to keep going and that whenever she messes up, to tell herself, "It's all good, Michelle! You're not there yet but you will be!" And her dad, well, he's the one who showed her all the moves:

"I'll never forget when I was learning harder scratches that I wanted to master, and when I struggled with them, Dad used to put his hand above mine, patiently and slowly showing me the patterns and the easiest way to tame them. Sometimes it wasn't so easy, but I refused to give up. I continued practicing until my fingers hurt."

When it comes to Michelle's musical tastes, she enjoys listening to . . .

"I guess I love it all! The classics. All the giants from the hip-hop world and R&B. Disco and rock music, too! But I also like contemporary stuff. I like it all, really. Especially when I can share my love of music with my friends. One of the greatest memories I have is when I performed at my friend's birthday party for the first time. I was only six! That was the best!"

"I remember myself standing on the deck, with kids and parents looking at me with admiration and waiting for the great party. Am I ready to repay their trust? Yes, I am! I'm ready to rock!" –DJM

Michelle's Faves!

"The first beat I scratched to was the instrumental break of a song called 'What's the Difference?' by Eminem and Dr. Dre. I still love scratching to it, but my scratches are much better now."

Favorite artist: Michael Jackson

Favorite song: "Dani California" by the Red Hot Chili Peppers and "Beat It" by Michael Jackson

"I know the lyrics of both songs by heart and love singing them. But that's not all. I could go on and on and on till the break of dawn!"

As a big fan, Michelle spent hours on trying to move like Michael Jackson. She thinks he is the best of the best!

Mixing

"The first skill I mastered, that every DJ must master, is called mixing. That means you blend two songs together, and it's what we do when we perform."

THERE ARE THREE MAIN STEPS:

1. Upload. You have to choose two songs when you start your DJ set. You play the first one, and then prepare the second one . . .

2. Match. All songs have BPM, which stands for "beats per minute." The BPM is basically the speed/tempo of the song. For example, Track A is 99 BPM and Track B is 103 BPM. You have to match the BPM of two songs by moving the pitch control fader either to plus or minus until both songs have the same BPM. It's kind of like having two friends going for a run, but one is faster and one is slower. If they're friends and they want to jog together, one of them will need to slow down or speed up so they can hang.

3. Mix. That's where the magic happens. The two songs blend. They talk to each other. Like old friends.

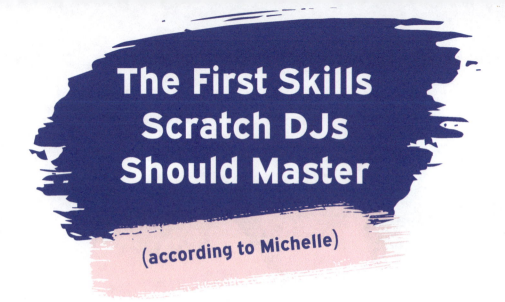

The First Skills Scratch DJs Should Master

(according to Michelle)

 A scratch DJ must learn the Baby Scratch first. That's when you move a record forward and backward, making a scratching sound. It's very easy to do. Easy enough for babies!

 After that, I learned some other cool scratching skills: **Chirp, Transformer, Stab, Boomerang, and Crab.**

 Chirp sounds precisely like a chirping bird. **Transformer** reminds me of when someone knocks on the door. **Stab** sounds to me like somebody cutting veggies on a board. **Boomerang** is like when someone opens and closes the door. And **Crab** got its name because when you move the cross-fader, your fingers look exactly like a walking crab.

 And now, when anybody asks me to teach them some beginner scratches, I show them these scratches first.

Let's admit that it still sounds really hard. Especially since she is using both hands at the same time. That's where things get really tricky. One hand is moving the cross-fader while the second hand pushes the records forward and backward.

Many adults can't even pat their head and rub their tummy at the same time. But we wouldn't be surprised if Michelle could do that while doing backflips. 🙂

"It's funny, because I used to do gymnastics! But music is my truest passion. Guess you could say that I'd like to be the Simone Biles of the DJ world. Best of the best of the best. Takes a clear mind and lots of practice, of course. But as my mom always says, 'practice makes perfect.'"

"I know, Mom, I know. Don't worry about me. I know people like to say that the sky is the limit. But why stop there! I'm going all the way to the galaxy! Can you dig it?"
—DJM 🙂

Mom? Or Momager?

When anybody asks Michelle about her mom's job, she proudly replies, **"SHE IS MY MOMAGER."**

Let's hand the mic over to Saida—Michelle's mom—for a second. We're dying to hear from one of Michelle's most important mentors!

What a great job she's done with Michelle!

"Michelle has always been very energetic, which is why she loves to perform. But not everyone who dabbles in music likes the stage. Some artists are really shy, and that's okay. There's more than one way to be an artist. And even though we celebrated all her talents, we didn't push her. In fact, we couldn't stop her. Even her preschool teachers noted that she adored music. She'd clap her hands the loudest during circle time and dance and sing as if she were already onstage, her long braids whipping about! Her favorite TV show to watch was *The Voice*, and after watching it she'd love to perform at home, too. Asking us to be the judges—judges who'd push the button and turn their seats to her every time."

"She always was ahead of her age, making everything look so easy to learn. Michelle is a combination of all our best traits. She is an upgraded version of us."

"She is a superstar, and what a privilege to be her parents and see her rise!"

"Back in Baku, we didn't expect she'd become a professional DJ. But we knew, without a doubt, that something magical was growing inside her. It's in everyone, of course. Once we were in Dubai, we could see that Michelle had it in spades!"

"I see myself on the biggest stage of Baku one day." —DJM 🙂

It's funny about Baku . . . Michelle always reminds her parents of things they've forgotten about, describing them in great detail. She remembers every toy and stuffie left behind. Every time they visit Baku, she makes a list of things she wants to bring back to Dubai.

Sometimes it's a toy she will never play with again, but one that instead serves as a souvenir of an early time in her childhood, of her motherland. She once had an idea to keep all the toys, games, and books she has ever owned—even if she has outgrown them—so that when she grows up, she can display them in a separate room that will be her little museum. In the end, she gave away most of the toys from Dubai, but she still keeps the most precious toys from Baku.

"DUBAI! WAIT FOR ME! I'M COMING!" —DJM 🙂

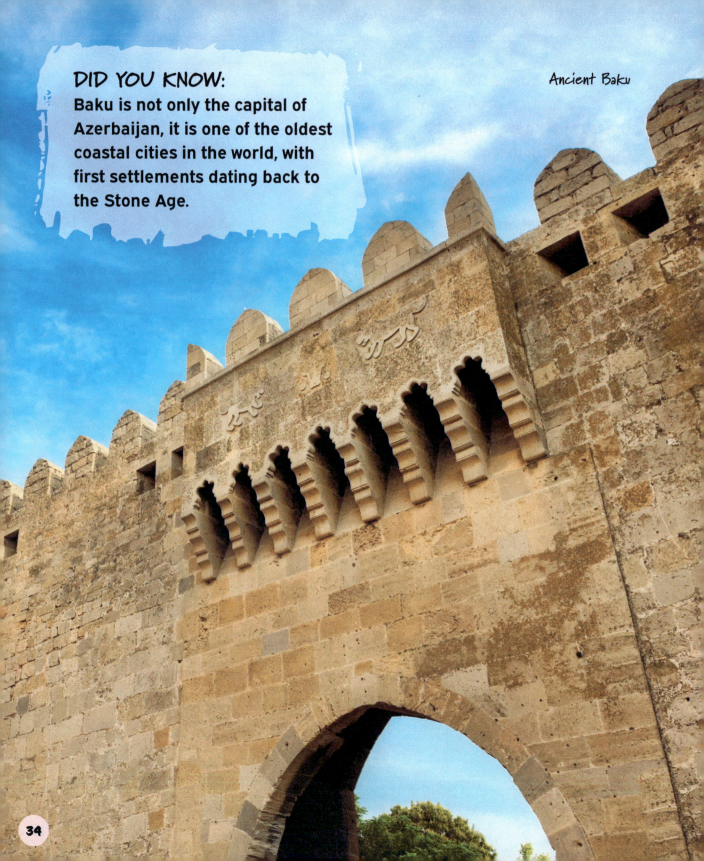

DID YOU KNOW:
Baku is not only the capital of Azerbaijan, it is one of the oldest coastal cities in the world, with first settlements dating back to the Stone Age.

Ancient Baku

Modern Dubai

wow

Baku is ancient. Dubai is brand new. Before 1958, when the UAE got into the oil business, Dubai was a dusty nowheresville. Then, all of a sudden, it was as if someone sprinkled magic glitter everywhere . . . up, up, up sprung a dazzling skyscraper forest and, *whoosh*, in flooded a sea of humanity—along with spectacular glowing fountains and a millionaires' row of manmade islands. If you google "Dubai world records," you'll find that it's home to the world's tallest building, the world's tallest chocolate sculpture, and the longest handmade gold chain. Being there, you can almost feel as if Dubai is putting on a show for you. It has the soul of a performer (a competitive one). So . . . what are we getting at? Nothing, other than it makes total sense that Dubai is where DJ Michelle decided to enter the 2021 World DMC competition—both to follow in Dad's footsteps and compete against him!

Practice and Influences

The roots of the turntablist style—and, in fact, hip-hop itself—can be traced back to a momentous date in music history: August 11, 1973. On that steamy summer afternoon, eighteen-year-old DJ Kool Herc (born Clive Campbell) hosted his first annual "Back to School Jam" at 1520 Sedgwick Avenue in the Bronx. At first, it was just another party for a good cause. He wanted to raise money for his little sister and other neighborhood kids so they could buy clothes for the coming school year. DJ Kool Herc began his set as usual, hunched over a microphone and two turntables, blasting funk by artists such as James Brown and Earth, Wind, and Fire. Nobody saw what was coming next. For the first time, he tried in public what he'd been practicing at home: breakbeats.

DJ Kool Herc took two copies of the same record and marked the beginning and end of a drum or instrumental section of a favorite song—a "break"—with masking tape on the vinyl. That way, he could keep the break going by creating a loop. When it came to the end on one turntable, he'd start it on the other, then back again . . . and on and on. The crowd went wild. With the beat pumping, he invited dancers to try out new moves. He handed over the mic to friends who freestyled poetry over the loop. Spinning, breakdancing, rapping—*hip-hop*—was born in a single day. What started as a party became a miracle.

After that first time performing live with her dad at the Dubai Mall, Michelle wanted to practice all day long.

But her dad had to slow her down. Teach her right.

FIGHT ME!

"Finally, I started getting good at all those buttons, knobs, faders, and cues that attracted me for so long. And I never wanted to leave the decks."
—DJM 😊

"Did I want to become a DJ the very first time I tried it out? Nooo, and you know why? Because in my mind, I already was a DJ!"
—DJM 😊

38

Part of being a professional DJ is knowing how to connect and handle the equipment, how to care for it so that it serves longer, and how and when to use certain settings. It is just as important as the art. It's like having a race car. If it breaks down, then you can't actually drive it! Equipment can let you down right in the middle of a performance. There can be a lot of reasons for that, even something as minor as high air temperature or humidity. The main thing Michelle's dad taught her is to keep calm and move on. Don't panic. Find a solution. Grab the microphone and talk to her audience. Keep the vibe and fix the problem.

"Once, five minutes before I was supposed to start my performance, something happened to the software and it didn't open. The only thing we could do was to delete the software and reinstall it—a process that could take more than five minutes. It was so upsetting. Luckily, I started my performance on time."

DJ Shock is no stranger to snafus. Once, the Dubai summer got too hot for his computer, and the program stopped working right at the beginning of his set. But he prepared in advance for just this sort of thing, so he could act immediately. He had copied all his music to a USB stick and played from that.

The best story is about an epic fail he had during a big performance for an audience of about a thousand. People were dancing and cheering. Michelle's dad was so thrilled to see the response of the crowd. And right at the peak of the party, he was flipping through his records for the right vinyl to play. When he found it, he got distracted and excited, anticipating the reaction on the dance floor. Instead of changing the record that wasn't playing, he grabbed the one on the spinning turntable and—*SCRAAATCH!* Sound impact! Music over! Everybody was shocked, including DJ Shock, but you couldn't tell by looking at him. He acted as if he'd planned it. And this is how he teaches Michelle to react if something goes wrong during her sets.

So, you could say that DJs are also problem fixers. Which is cool because the world has all sorts of problems and problems need fixers. Especially the fun and creative and patient kind, don't you think?

The world needs to listen to its artists and its fixers. And the fact that Michelle's dad taught her how to work with the equipment, how to respect and care for it—well, that sounds very important.

DJ Q*BERT

"Sure is! It's all digitalized now— we use computers when we DJ. So we take the best of the old and the new and make magic. But some DJs, like DJ Q*bert, still use classic turntables and original vinyls, which is also super cool."

40

For those who don't know who DJ Q*bert is, he's Michelle's hero! If you asked her and other scratch DJs to name their biggest influence—the one person they associate with the advanced scratching, the *master* scratching—they would all say Q*bert. All the DJs who are serious in scratching want to reach Q*bert's level.

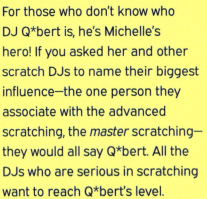

"Dad and I had Q*bert's photo placed right above the DJ setup at Dad's home studio in Baku. And you know what? We have a slip mat and mixer with his autograph as well. It's so inspiring."

41

"DJ Q*bert took scratching to the next level, which is why my dad calls him a sensei. And he is the inventor of some of the coolest scratches. Everybody thinks he is from another planet. He has a unique style nobody can repeat. And, what I admire the most about him is that even though he started scratching at the age of fifteen, he still has the same passion for it today. He will wake up at three a.m. and go straight to the turntables, scratching for real until the break of dawn . . . He goes for hours without breaks. He's dedicated his life to the art of DJing!"

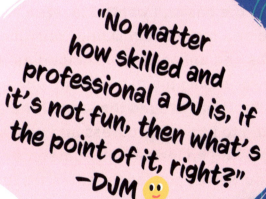

"No matter how skilled and professional a DJ is, if it's not fun, then what's the point of it, right?" —DJM

Another important pro tip from Michelle's dad was how to manage her music library and create playlists. He taught Michelle that it's better to decide what tracks to play *during* the event, not ahead of time—because only this way can you see the crowd's reaction to your music, and it will inspire you to make the right decisions. You are free to use the songs you think will work better for them in that exact moment. If you want to bring the heat to the show and keep the energy high, you need to be able to adapt your set and use your knowledge of music. It's all about feeling—feeling your audience, feeling their vibe.

So a DJ is only as good as their talents and equipment—and *also* their ability to connect with people.

Problem fixers, collaborators, creative thinkers, good-vibe spreaders... This is exactly what the world needs! But aside from learning from her dad, what other tools of learning does Michelle often use? Let's find out!

"If you ask me, that is what DJing is about: having fun, spreading good vibes, and lifting people up—right in front of you."
—DJM

"The internet! After my dad taught me all the basics, I wanted to learn more and more about DJing. YouTube videos and online schools helped me a lot. I kept surprising my dad with my fast and flashy results. That's around the same time that we also started to film my progress and post videos of me playing on Instagram. Sometimes we'd film ourselves playing together. It's funny, though, my dad, Mr. Professional—the one who really got me into this—doesn't like cameras! But that's okay because I love to film and do that kind of techy stuff on my own, too. And now we teach each other things and work on improving our skills *together*. Like beat juggling and drumming skills. Sometimes I like to learn the advanced beat juggles first, and then I break it down to him. He's a good student!"

COOL!

DJ Q*BERT

44

DJ HEROES

Michelle's other battle DJ heroes are DJ Craze, A-Trak, and DJ Rob Swift. The first thing she learned about DJ Craze is that he won the DMC World DJ Championships three times over, three years in a row! For twenty years, it was a record nobody could beat until DJ Skillz tied him in 2020 with three consecutive wins. On top of that, DJ Craze is one of very few DJs in the world who can scratch equally well with both left and right hands, which is super difficult.

"I remember the first time seeing one of Michelle's videos and thinking, *WOAH!* 🐵 This lil girl is way ahead of her time. She has that fire that will make her one of the greats. I'm always proud and impressed every time I see her videos. The future of turntablism is in good hands with Michelle! Mad love and respect. 🙏" —DJ Craze

"His routines, which he prepares for several months, just can't be replicated due to how difficult they are and how much skill they require! I noticed that every new routine he creates becomes more and more difficult, which means he never stops growing even though it seems he couldn't be any better. And what I really love about Craze is that he does so much. He plays international club gigs and is also a producer, which is rare among battle DJs."

A-Trak won the DMC World DJ Championship at the age of fifteen, making him the youngest winner of the competition at that time! He was also the first DJ to win all three major DJ competition titles—DMC, ITF, and Vestax—as well as the first DJ to win five World Championships! On top of his other projects, A-Trak was Kanye West's tour DJ and worked closely with him. He is also known because of his original music and remixes, and together with Armand Van Helden he is a part of the Duck Sauce DJ duo, which was nominated for a Grammy in 2011 for their song "Barbra Streisand."

#INSPIRATION

"The first thing that most people notice about DJ Michelle is probably her young age, along with her skill level. But what strikes me is how much she already covers all the aspects of DJing. The job of the DJ is to provide a good time and to control the vibe of a party. When people see Michelle play, they smile, they get in a good mood, they feel something contagious. Yes, she also works hard, and yes, she has quickly mastered a lot of technique, but what I love the most is the way she makes people feel!" —A-Trak

"So just imagine how great he is! On top of all his other achievements, he is also a founder of the annual Goldie Awards—an invitational DJ competition that I was lucky enough to be a part of. I became the youngest participant and a finalist in 2021's competition!"

And of course, there's DJ Rob Swift, also known as Brolic Arm, who helped invent turntablism from the very beginning. He's worked with everyone from Linkin Park to the Red Hot Chili Peppers and Herbie Hancock. He was part of a revolutionary scratching group that was world-famous in the nineties—the X-Ecutioners.

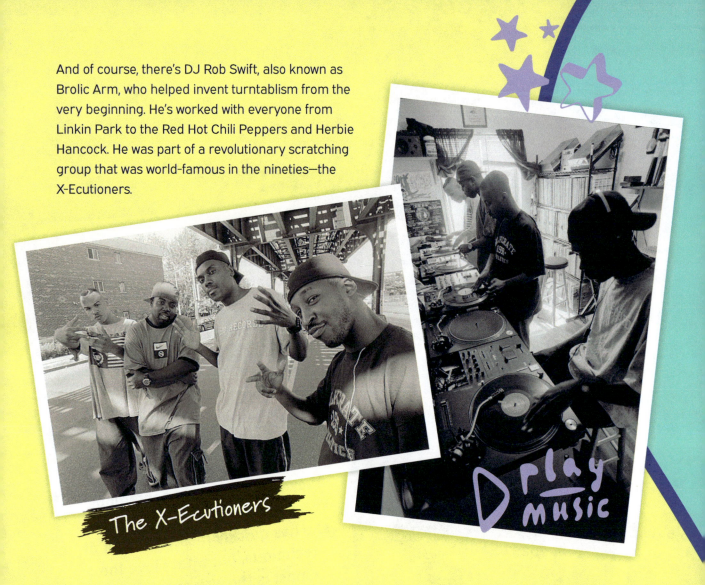

The X-Ecutioners

"For me, he is the best beat juggler and the best beat-juggling teacher ever, and I feel so honored to be a part of Brolic Army—his online DJ school. Rob Swift once said that DJing gives him purpose and helped him create a way to feel useful to people. And what I really appreciate is that he not only teaches the techniques but also the history of hip-hop: scratching, DJing, and beat juggling—to pay respect to the people who created the skills that make up what DJing is today."

"When we think about modern-day DJ greats, it's often people who are making an impact on our art form as adults. But young people can, and often do, influence the trajectory of DJing in positive ways. DJ Michelle is one of those young people . . . Michelle's ability to grasp techniques and concepts that take the average adult years to master is alone impressive. But what I appreciate most about this young DJ prodigy is you can tell she's embraced DJing because it's fun for her. It's the fun aspect of this art form that motivated pioneers like Grandmaster Flash and Grand Wizzard Theodore to scratch and juggle on turntables in the first place. Today, Michelle stands as an example that as far removed from the formative years of Hip Hop, and DJing specifically, as she is, she can still help push it further. Showcasing its artistry to her young peers, therefore ensuring the growth of DJing for years to come!"

—DJ Rob Swift

DID YOU KNOW:
DJ Rob Swift has his own online DJ school, Brolic Army. You can check them out (and even register) at BrolicArmyDJSchool.com. Naturally, it is based in Queens, Rob Swift's home and the birthplace of hip-hop.

DJ Rob Swift

Sounds like Michelle knows a lot of that history of hip-hop herself! And here is how she explains where her interest in the history of DJing comes from:

"I have to know where a genius like Q*bert came from and how he came up. The contributions he and other legends made to the art of DJing are impossible to list in one place. They're all retired from competitions now, freeing the way for the younger generation. I'm just glad they still perform, that they showcase their turntable skills, thrilling the world—and me—with their creations.

"I'll just add one thing: I cannot talk about the history of DJing without mentioning the documentary *Scratch*. It features DJ Q*bert and DJ Rob Swift as well. And it's so much more than a story about musicians and turntablists. It's about a revolution in music—about the birth of hip-hop, about the invention of scratching and beat juggling, and the endless possibilities of vinyl. The first time I saw it, I remember being so grateful for the opportunity to learn from the pioneers themselves. Personally, it's really important for me to know the roots of turntablism, and this documentary became one of the biggest influences I ever had. You might ask me how I found out about this film—my parents, of course! It was made before I was born!"

The Gear behind the Music

The very first piece of equipment Michelle owned, which she got for her fifth birthday when she decided to become a DJ—specifically, a *world-famous* DJ—was the Pioneer SX DJ Controller. She used it to play at her first gigs.

On this controller, Michelle learned beatmatching, mixing, and how to use software. After she learned basics on the controller, she started to play on her dad's equipment. The videos they posted of these moments marked the first time Michelle went viral! Celebrities such as Chris Brown, DJ Snake, and Soulja Boy were the first who reposted and commented about how talented she was.

Features to master:

Crossfader
This tool helps you switch from one song to another very quickly and helps to cut samples while you are scratching.

Performance Pads
These help you to manage position of the track and allow you to create toneplays, which can be used as transitions or just as a creative mixing technique.

FX Buttons and Filters
These help create a vibe!

"Turntables and a mixer allowed me to learn scratching and beat juggling!"
—DJM

"I like using effects, especially Echo, when mixing and switching the songs."
—DJM

The next phase was really remarkable. At just seven years old, Michelle was picked to be a Brand Ambassador to the UAE. The Numark company has local distributors who noticed Michelle on social media. Soon their representatives approached the family with the proposal to meet at their office. "We met and discussed the opportunity with the team, and the next time we saw them we were ready to sign the contract! Michelle put her own brand sign next to her dad's, with a big smile on her face," Michelle's mom explained.

It was a very exciting time—Michelle's first contract with a big brand, and the distinction of being the youngest Numark Brand Ambassador ever!

54

As part of the deal, Michelle received her very own Numark PT01 Portable Turntables and Numark Scratch Mixer for use at home, and a Numark Mixtrack Platinum FX controller for mobile DJing.

"The portable turntable allows me to continue practicing scratching even when I am outside or traveling."
—DJM

2021 was a level up! Numark's parent company, inMusic, saw Michelle's worldwide success and her rapid professional growth, and they decided to make Michelle a Global RANE Artist. She received RANE Twelve motorized turntables, a RANE Seventy-Two MKII mixer, which she uses at home, and a RANE One Professional Motorized DJ Controller, which she uses at her gigs.

"When you do what you love, luck awaits you every step of the way." —DJM 😊

Michelle notes that turntables are too heavy to transport to every venue. Plus, it takes longer to connect them and to get ready, and they take up more space in a DJ booth.

"If the venue provides me with turntables, that's great. Of course, I prefer to perform on those. But if not, RANE One is the best solution. It has all the features I need to mix and scratch as I do on two turntables, but it's compact and mobile."

Michelle doesn't use real vinyls for the gigs. Performing on real vinyl is riskier and can ruin the set. They are so sensitive to all sorts of factors, like bass vibrations and especially the weather. Since she is still too young to perform at the clubs—and will be for a while—her big gigs are always in open-air venues, which is why she must always think about the weather's impact.

Kudos again to Michelle's mom and dad for being such fabulous teachers. Did they have a plan or regimen when they began teaching Michelle about music? Come on, it's time for us to get to know a little more. Let's see what her mom has to say about her early years.

"We didn't have a special regimen when we started. Everything was happening randomly. We taught her whenever we had free time and were ready to begin anytime she said yes. When you start scratching, your fingers get tired really quickly, especially if you are a kid with those cute little hands. Of course, when that happens you have to have a break. So at first it was just three- or five-minute sessions during the day. But as time went on and she became serious, we set a goal to scratch fifteen minutes a day. We felt that was ideal at the beginning, so she wouldn't get too tired, but there was still routine and consistency. We didn't stick to this plan too strictly, though, because Michelle has always had a lot of hobbies and interests. Sometimes it wasn't possible to fit everything she wanted to do in a whole day. So every now and then she would skip practice altogether. We wanted her to be driven only by her interest and passion, not by us."

She is full of energy and can do a lot in a day.

Also, because her dad was at the turntables every day, Michelle was always indirectly involved in the process. As her parents realized later, she wasn't just watching him do his thing; she was absorbing it—memorizing his hand and body moves, patterns, and other details. Even when she was busy with something else, her ears listened and took notes. So if she skipped her own practice time, she still soaked up her dad's DJing like a sponge. Michelle's parents would often be amazed when she got back behind the turntables because it was as if she'd been practicing hard all along without any break at all.

As Michelle's mom and dad watched her talent blossom, they didn't know if they should push for even more extraordinary results—the stage parent way—or let her continue following her own course and see what happened. She learns so fast and makes everything look so easy, and they've always wondered what she could achieve if she spent several hours a day on the deck, the way professional pianists spend four to five hours playing piano. Here is what Michelle's mom has to say about it:

"But then we remember what matters. She is not just a celebrity, the youngest girl DJ in the world. She is our daughter. The most important thing for us is to see her happy. So we chose a middle road. We continue giving her freedom to decide how she wants to spend her day. At the same time, we guide and encourage her, reminding her of the gift of talent she was given and how special she is. In fact, her obsession with music is so strong that our reminders were unnecessary. More recently, inspirational books have fostered her passion even more, serving as a finishing touch. Her favorite is *You Are Awesome* **by Matthew Syed; she has read it several times and returns to it over and over again."**

59

GOING PRO

"DJ Michelle is a born entertainer and skilled musician with the gifts that keep giving! It is a pleasure to watch this turntable angel grow and continually bless all our souls!" —DJ Q*bert

Like DJ Michelle, DJ Q*bert—a.k.a. Richard Quitevis—fell in love with music as a toddler. His parents gave him a plastic Fisher-Price record player before he was even a kindergartener! He played his first professional gig with a single turntable and a cheap Radio Shack mixer and never looked back. By twenty he had cofounded the legendary Invisibl Skratch Piklz, the first all-DJ band. Now a DMC Hall of Fame inductee, twice voted DMC World Champion (in 1992 and 1993), Q*bert humbly credits God for creating his scratching techniques. These include the Laser, the Phaser, the Hydroplane, the Squid, and . . . well, too many to list here. You can find them in his book, *Scratchlopedia Breaktannica: 100 Secret Scratches*, though he claims the number is closer to one thousand. It makes perfect sense that he wrote a book on the subject, as he often compares scratches to words—each one a part of his psychedelic vocabulary.

Michelle is a curious kid, who wants to try everything and finds inspiration everywhere. And it's no wonder that she quickly decided to take her DJing to the next level and start producing. How does she find the time to fit it all in? Is there anything she can't do?

"I started producing right after my parents took me to the Dubai Apple Store a couple of years ago for a GarageBand workshop for kids. GarageBand is like having a little recording studio on your computer or iPad or iPhone. I've since read that some big names in the industry have used it for their official albums and hit songs. Isn't that incredible?"

DID YOU KNOW? According to the official online GarageBand Guide, Rihanna, Radiohead, and Trent Reznor are just some of the big names who've used the program to create their bestselling albums.

GarageBand has a template for beginners. So if you want to make a hip-hop beat, the hip-hop templates help with that. They're like training wheels, and eventually, when you are ready, you can ride solo, making your own original music. Michelle has now moved to other software with more powerful features, like Ableton Live—which her dad also uses, along with some of the best music producers and DJs making music today.

"I started with simple reggaeton and hip-hop beats, but recently my dad taught me how to do mashups." —DJM

61

Mackie gear supported DJ Michelle with equipment for producing!

DID YOU KNOW?
Mashups are when you blend two or more songs, normally by overlaying the acapella of one track seamlessly over the instrumental of another track, changing the tempo and key if it's necessary.

"It wasn't long before I created my first two mashups—Tiësto's 'The Business' with the Black-Eyed Peas' 'Vida Loca,' and BTS's 'Butter' with Nina Sky's 'Move Ya Body'—and I love seeing people's reaction when I play them during performances. I feel so happy to see that they love it."
—DJM

Road to Fame

As the youngest professional girl DJ, Michelle is followed by hundreds of thousands of fans. But, speaking of fans, when did people first start hearing about her? Michelle has a story to tell:

"**The thing that helped me get noticed was Instagram. We regularly posted my wordplays, toneplays, and scratching videos showing my progress. As it's so unusual for kids at my age to do what I was doing, I started getting the attention of big celebrities, receiving more and more views, getting more and more followers and first-booking requests.**"

Michelle's first autograph

MEGA

"People started recognizing me and approaching me, telling me that they are big fans of mine. Incredible feeling! I remember when I gave my first ever autograph. I wasn't even ready for that and didn't have an exact autograph yet! He promised: 'I'll keep it safe, because I know you'll get super famous very soon.' And I believed him."

Check it out

DJ Michelle's social media handle is
@IAmDJMichelle

And if you saw Michelle DJing on Instagram and Facebook, check out her TikTok account! You will find funny daddy-daughter videos with millions of views!

Turns out that guy who wanted her autograph was right. Amazing! But we're getting ahead of ourselves. It's time to hear about how Michelle started performing for an audience in the first place. What was it like? How did she feel? And when the time came for her to perform, was she nervous? We all know that feeling when hands and feet get all jittery. Did it get the best of her? Or did she just push through it all?

After performing at friends' birthday parties and other kids' events, Michelle felt she was ready to step onto the bigger stage. And the perfect opportunity presented itself when she won a talent competition in a social media contest! As a result, she got the chance to perform for a bigger audience at the Jumeirah Beach stage during the Dubai Food Festival!

"It was an amazing experience. The weather was perfect, and I remember looking at all the joyful and happy people. If they were too far away from the stage, they could watch me on the big screen installed behind me. Everything went so perfectly. I proved to myself and everybody else that I was ready to rock the big stages, too! I love watching the video from that day—it brings those incredible emotions rolling back. It was all the feels! And just so awesome, like what I imagine surfing a big wave would feel like. I was the surfer, the music my board, and the audience was the waves. It all works together."

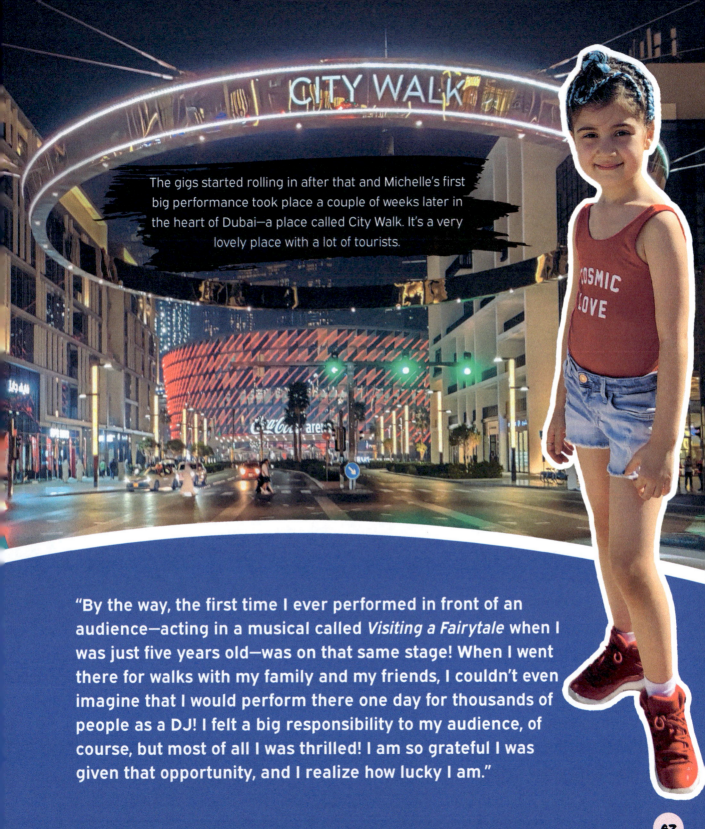

The gigs started rolling in after that and Michelle's first big performance took place a couple of weeks later in the heart of Dubai—a place called City Walk. It's a very lovely place with a lot of tourists.

"By the way, the first time I ever performed in front of an audience—acting in a musical called *Visiting a Fairytale* when I was just five years old—was on that same stage! When I went there for walks with my family and my friends, I couldn't even imagine that I would perform there one day for thousands of people as a DJ! I felt a big responsibility to my audience, of course, but most of all I was thrilled! I am so grateful I was given that opportunity, and I realize how lucky I am."

DJ Michelle Is Playing for You!

"I remember I got up really early in the morning because I was afraid to be late—even though I wasn't due onstage until the evening. I must have checked the equipment we were supposed to take with us a thousand times, just to be sure nothing was missing. Finally, it was time to leave! We knew we needed to get to the venue well in advance because we had to do a sound check. I barely remember that part of it, because the first thing that I saw when we arrived was a giant poster with my photo on it— **DJ MICHELLE IS PLAYING FOR YOU!**"

"Unbelievable! I wondered: *Is that even me?* For the first time, I felt famous—like a big star! A real celebrity! Especially when the crowd started pouring in. I knew there would be a lot of people, but I didn't know it would be that big. Kids and parents were asking to take a photo with me before they even saw me perform. I just kept thinking, *Wow!***"**

So she was waiting at the side of the stage when the MC made the announcement: "Our youngest DJ will start to play in just five minutes!" *It's time!* she thought, but Michelle says she didn't have stage fright. She had then what she's always had before a performance ever since: flying butterflies in her stomach. She calls this feeling *excinervousness* (excitement + nervousness). And no matter if it's her first performance or millionth the excinervousness is always there.

"Performing on the big stage was my dream! No matter how many stages I conquer, this first time I will cherish the most!"
—DJM 🙂

And what helps Michelle to manage it is . . .

"Jumping! Jumping and dancing! I have to move the big parts of me and the little parts—like my fingers and toes. I have to let the energy out or it will get all tangled up inside of me. But everyone has a different approach. Some people get pumped by listening to loud music, others meditate and relax. What works for me is jumping. It helps me to melt away the nervousness, keep the right amount of excitement, and feel fully warmed up before taking the stage. And the icing on the cake? I have a secret handshake with my parents!"

69

A secret handshake! That is fantastic. We'd ask for more, but then it wouldn't be secret! But do tell us more about how you prepare yourself. It would help others when they are trying out something new—*anything* new—that makes them nervous.

"Have you ever tried visualization? That's what I do. I close my eyes, take in a couple of deep breaths—in and out, and in and out—and then I visualize myself on the big stage, rocking it, rocking the crowd, having a fantastic performance. Visualizing the best scenario in your head and talking to yourself in a positive way when preparing for the gig . . . it's always a good idea."

"If you don't believe in yourself and don't see yourself as a star, nobody else can either. You must be your number one supporter. You cheer yourself on to be as cool as you want to be."
—DJM

"With practice and the support I get from my parents, these steps help me to get any unwanted feelings out of my head and be confident with myself, my skills, and my ability to shine in a performance."

To be prepared physically, Michelle rehearses at home. She loves to create an audience during these home rehearsals—and as she has a small family, she uses her stuffed animals to play the role of the crowd.

She even has a big DJ teddy bear in her audience. He tells her if she needs to improve some technical part of a performance.

AWW!!!

But she doesn't practice a lot before the event, because over-practicing can make her feel tired before even getting to the stage.

"I have as many rehearsals as I need to feel prepared and ready."

As a performer, you will always feel more confident if you look good. If you want to be a star, you should look and feel like a star first, so the outfit is an important part of the show.

"I have my own style—I always wear something on my head—a cap, a hat, a beanie, or a bandana. So even if I play at home, I always wear my cap and my 'show clothes.' It helps me to teleport myself to the big stage, to feel and control the excitement, and to focus. I know that people pay attention to everything, including your appearance and the way you move, the way you look at them from the stage, and the way you interact with them. If you share some love and do your best to make them happy, it will show them how significant *they* are to *you*. Both during my home rehearsals and stage performances I do my best to entertain my homies and have a great time with them."

So let's get back to the gig and see how she felt when she started...

"Once I stepped on the stage and heard all the people cheering and clapping, I felt something more than just those butterflies . . . it was an incredible sensation that I still can't find the right words to describe! I looked at the crowd. And I knew that I was doing something valuable. It taught me always to be incredibly thankful for the support and kindness of people who enjoy my work and feel happy when I play for them. It's big. It's so big . . ."

So that day, after putting on the last track of her set, she went to the front part of the stage to be closer to the audience—to show them how much they meant to her . She danced till the end of the song. That was something unexpected, and everybody loved it!

75

After her set, Michelle went offstage to greet her friends and take photos with her fans. When it was all over, she turned to her parents and said, "Mom, Dad, can we repeat all this again tomorrow?"

If you want to be a famous DJ, you realize that stage performances are a big part of your musical journey. And it's better to be as prepared as you can be, both technically and emotionally.

And there is one more thing that helps Michelle to feel and see herself as a superstar before getting to the stage!

"I have my own 'rider,' as all the big stars do. Before every performance, my dad buys me something special. I get to decide what it will be—a huge Lego set, a book series, Funko Pop figures, vinyl records, Rubik's Cubes, or other things I currently have on my wish list. I know celebrities all have their own riders, and I guess that's mine! It's all about the little things that make you happy and feel special, you know? It helps me feel ready to have fun and share the fire that burns within me! So that I'm ready to channel those Tiësto vibes."

She sounds like a pro, doesn't she?

DID YOU KNOW?

Tiësto is arguably one of the most famous and successful DJs on the planet. When interviewed in 2017 on the CNN show In the Booth, he was asked if his grueling lifestyle was glamorous. The short answer was yes. But getting to that answer required sticking to some principles:

- Take care of yourself.
- Practice every day.
- Listen and learn from others.
- Do it for the music—not the money.
- And above all, remember what matters most: the love you have for your friends and your family.

Shortly after that first impromptu performance with her dad at the Dubai Mall, he sat her down in their living room and told her how much he believed in her.

"He told me I had what it takes to go pro! I jumped up and down on the couch and looked again at all those posters on our walls—all the hip-hop greats—and it felt like they were winking at me. Nodding in agreement. Like, 'Hey, girl! You've got this. Welcome to the fam!'"

"I am a world-famous DJ at heart and the sooner the world knows about it, the better!" —DJM

★★★

Let's check in with Mom now, to see how she and Michelle's dad felt about their daughter's first show.

"We had all the feelings! But our family motto is positivity. With positive thinking, your mind is already in the right place to deal with whatever comes your way. But she's still a kid, after all, and we knew that a thousand different things could have gone wrong with her performance. So we did worry a bit. What if something happened that she'd never dealt with before? What if she got confused and froze like a deer? What if she didn't like the big crowd, or, worse yet, what if the big crowd didn't like her?"

What if, what if, what if . . .

"But eventually you have to pull back from what if and return to your training and your passion. And for us, that means returning to our positive mindset."

Michelle's mom recalls their game plan: They arrived very early for sound check and to walk the stage—it is good to get to know your surroundings before you play. Then they took their places. Michelle's dad stayed behind Michelle, backstage, to help with technical matters. Her mom took the front row to film and be a familiar face for Michelle to see. And soon the crowd started coming, and the show began. Her mom recalls those first moments:

"When Michelle walked across the stage my heart leapt. So, for a second, all I could hear was my heart pounding. But when the crowd roared and the music started, the anxiety vanished. I knew that she was enjoying herself just by looking at her eyes. She was on fire.

"That day I was less of a 'momager' than a listener. And when the show ended and I finally got to see her big, beautiful brown eyes and she hugged me, I understood everything before she even got a word out.

"'The stage is my home,' she said, squeezing me.

"A tear fell from my eyes. I was so proud. I'd be proud of her no matter what, but music is everything. To gift it to others is very special, indeed."

"I can't believe our small family parties have grown into something big like this in no time! Bravo, Michelle!" —MOM

79

A DAY IN HER LIFE

In interviews, professional DJs are often asked to describe a typical day. The answer tends to be the same, whether from global celebrities to rising stars to underground legends: every day is different, and no day is ever easy. Regardless of how many fans they may have, a DJ's life is spent behind the turntables, traveling from gig to gig, sleeping at odd hours, and balancing long stretches of calmness with the sudden spotlight. A day can go from ordinary to triumphant in the span of a few hours . . . and then you have to wake up and do it all over again.

It's hard to remember that as Michelle writes this book, she is only ten years old. And it's so interesting to learn what her typical day looks like.

"I guess my typical day isn't much different than anyone else's. What I do depends on a lot of things—whether it's school time or holidays, or whether it's too hot in Dubai to go outside. If it's school time, then I design my day around studying. And normally the first thing I do in the morning after having my breakfast is my lessons. But did you notice that I said how my day starts *normally*? It means it's not always like that."

Let's start with the fun stuff, then. On a holiday when the weather is fine, Michelle likes spending time in the dog park where dog owners from the whole neighborhood bring their pets for a walk.

"Did I mention that I'm a dog person? I have over a hundred dog friends! I adore playing with them—tossing around balls or sticks, playing tag, rolling around in the grass, doing tricks . . . just hugging and having fun with them."
—DJM

When it's too hot outside, she mostly spends her time in the pool. Swimming is one of Michelle's favorite sports, and she tries to do twenty laps every time she goes in, with five laps for each stroke—freestyle, breaststroke, backstroke, and even the most difficult one: butterfly!

Music-wise, if she's not doing her DJ thing, then she's singing to rock songs and playing drums or her bass guitar, which she named. It's called Mike—after Flea from Red Hot Chili Peppers, one of Michelle's favorite bands. Off the stage, Flea is Michael Balzary. Onstage he's a bundle of nonstop energy, just like she is.

Flea

DID YOU KNOW?

Like DJ Michelle, Flea grew up in a musical home. His stepfather, Walter Urban, was a professional jazz musician who hosted jam sessions at their home in Los Angeles. Flea has something else in common with DJ Michelle: he didn't begin his musical journey with the bass. His first instrument was the trumpet. You can hear his trumpet-playing on Jane's Addiction's "Idiots Rule."

"I'm a big reader, thanks to my mom. She read to me all the time when I was little. I used to memorize the stories my mom and grandma would read to me back in Baku. If they missed a word, I would correct them and giggle a bit. And when I learned to read on my own, I read every day because I couldn't get enough. I felt like the characters were my real friends. Sort of like the musicians on the posters at home. In my mind, we are all part of the same family," says Michelle.

"My favorite books are the Harry Potter series by J. K. Rowling and the Inheritance Cycle by Christopher Paolini. I just love a good story. I love to watch them, too."

FUN FACT!

Michelle is also passionate about learning languages. She is fluent in English, and now she's determined to learn German. She also knows a little French, Azerbaijani, Arabic, Spanish, Chinese, and Japanese. "Music is the best language there is. It crosses borders and builds friendships. In fact, I can't think of anything better than enjoying music with my family and friends by my side," she states.

"And, big surprise, both of my favorite movies are about dogs! *Hachi: A Dog's Tale* and *A Dog's Purpose*. The first one is based on a true story about an Akita Inu found in a train station. The man who finds him decides to keep him because nobody seems to be looking for him. Over time, the man trains the dog and they form a beautiful bond, and Hachiko starts to wait for him to get off the train after work every day. When the man passes away, Hachiko keeps returning to the train station at five o'clock sharp—every day for nine years until his own death. Sad but sweet. *A Dog's Purpose* is about a boy named Ethan and a dog named Bailey who have a special bond. Bailey dies, but he's reborn again and again with a new look, until finally one day he reunites with his best friend, who is now a lonely old man. Bailey finds his purpose in uniting Ethan with Hannah, and they live out the rest of their days happy together."

"My ultimate, ultimate dream is to hang out with all my dog friends from the dog park, watch dog movies together, and then jam to music with them! Do you think Harry Potter's magic wand could help me with that?"
—DJM

SCHOOL DAYS

The calmest mornings start with studying or reading. But there are also mornings when Michelle wakes up her parents with the noise of the fader—even if she's wearing headphones. It clicks while she's scratching. Still other days, her parents rouse to the sound of her voice and amplifier as she sings and strums her bass or hits the drums . . . Michelle confides that her dad makes just as much noise as she does, but usually later in the day. For this reason, they always live in corner apartments, preferably set apart from others as much as possible. "That way," Michelle says, "our neighbors can sleep in peace in the morning and have peaceful days. But if you come close to our door, you will nearly always hear the sound of music. *Great* music."

School was so different these past couple of years because of COVID-19. But Michelle feels that she is so lucky to be studying online and to have a flexible schedule. She can start whenever she wants, and she can also allow herself to take breaks and have some fun between the lessons. She prefers to finish her lessons as fast as possible and then dedicate the remaining time to DJing, her other hobbies, and to her friends. Sometimes she finishes school before her parents even wake up in the morning—she loves waking up really early—so she has the whole day at her disposal, spent with music and family. They love listening to their favorite tunes, dancing and singing all together, and seeking out new releases and rare remixes to add to their music library, enlarging their collection and keeping it up to date.

"Of course, even on school days, I always spend some time on the decks," she says, **"perfecting my skills, learning something new, thinking up a new routine and then filming it . . . There is always something new to learn and so much to do—behind-the-scenes work that hides under that one perfect DJ set or a short social media post you might watch. Creativity takes me other places, too. Like playing chess with Dad, playing other board games, solving a Rubik's Cube, doing puzzles, building and playing with Lego sets—the list goes on. Remember the rider I told you about? That's to feed those hobbies! Besides, since I love stories, I also love writing them."**

And here's one she wrote for school, a true story called

"Vihr and Me."

I sat inside the tiny, dim room that I'd be calling my home for a few days. Today, we'd be going to a farm. I really wanna see horses—they're my favorite animals, as well as dogs, parrots, turtles, and dolphins. Back in the days when I was little, I used to have tons of horse figurines and I played "Farm" almost every day!

"Michelle! Time to go!" I heard my dad shouting.

"Coming," I answer, getting up from the rug in front of the TV, where I was watching *Harry Potter*. I pull on my jeans and shirt—ideal wear for the farm—step into my sneakers, wear my old cowboy "hatty," as I call it, and meet my parents at the door.

"The driver's calling, he must be waiting," Mum says. I nod and press the "DOWN" button and the elevator doors slide open slowly. I press "G," and we get there in a few seconds. Then, I see Mr. Driver (I don't know his name) and his big, black car waiting outside.

We've been driving for nearly half an hour already. I start moaning, "I hate lo-o-ong car rides like this . . ." I feel like I'm going to be sick any moment now. The car finally pulls up near a sign saying, "FARM AHEAD." I step out and take a big breath of fresh air. A woman greets us. "G'day!" She pronounces. She looks like a cowgirl. I answer, "Hi," and grin.

"Okay, so here are the goats," says the farmer woman, and she points at a field near a barn. I try not to breathe as we pass it, because it smells d-i-s-g-u-s-t-i-n-g. Then I see a baby goat snoozing near the barn and forget all about it. "Aww," I croon. The farmer disappears into the barn house for a moment and then comes back with a bottle of milk—it looks as if she's about to feed a newborn baby. "Take this; you can feed 'em babies," she says, throwing the bottle to me. I catch it, but some milk drips down on the grass. The baby goat looks up, aware of the yummy milk bottle in my hand. She rises and roughly pushes her tiny (but v-e-r-y sharp) horns into my leg. I wince, but then lower the milk bottle and the baby goat starts sucking. She drains half the bottle immediately, and I pull it away from her. "Whoa, hungry, aren't you?" I say and start running, the bottle gripped tightly in my hand. The baby goat starts following, and I get tired out very soon. I stop, raising the bottle up over my head. The baby goat props its front hooves on my chest and jumps up, knocking the bottle out of my hand . . .

I have so much fun. I go visit the chickens, who go extreme if I try and even get close, the geese, who are v-e-r-y rude and try and bite me, the rabbits, the cows, everything! And now, we were, last but not least, going to visit the HORSES! The part I've been anxiously waiting for THE MOST! We enter the stables. I run to the nearest horse—her name was Natasha. As I get closer, Natasha gives out an enormous SNEEZE, and I get so scared that I jump back and collide with another door. I look up and see that the door bears a giant sign: "CAREFUL, I BITE!" I move away from it just as a horse the size of a building (that's what I thought) looms into view. I go through every door and at last, I see a beautiful horse standing in the end. It's light brown, with a jet-black mane and tail—it's simply GORGEOUS!

"What's his name?" I ask the farmer.

"His name is Vihr," she answers.

"He's the best!" I say.

Nervously I sit down on the saddle, which was placed on Vihr's back. This is the first time I have ever ridden a horse. The farmer woman explains the correct position and gives Vihr the signal to "Go!" She walks beside us as I ride a few laps, and then she stops, so that Vihr and I ride on our own.

It's time to go. We're heading straight to the airport from the farm, so we've got to hurry. I hug Vihr and whisper to him, "Vihr, promise me, you'll wait here until I come back. It'll be very soon. I love you, boy . . . goodbye . . ." And we go. I feel like I'm going to cry.

From that day on, I dream of getting my own horse, and when I do, I'm going to name him after my new best friend. Vihr will stay in my memory forever.

True Friends are Never Appart

That definitely doesn't sound like a typical day, either. Here is another moment in Michelle's life where she had to say goodbye to her best friend. She hopes her story will help others who are experiencing the same right now to feel better and know they're not alone:

"One of the saddest moments in my life was when I heard the news that my best friend Amalia was leaving Dubai. It seemed impossible to me. What would we do without each other? I couldn't stop crying, the happy moments flashing before my eyes. It only got worse and worse until the day finally came. We said goodbye and hugged each other. If you live in a multinational city like Dubai, you can never say your friendship is forever. Usually, people come here to work a little and then return to their home countries afterward. The most difficult thing to accept is that one day it could happen to you and your best friend.

"My mom always says there is a way out of any situation, but I didn't see any. I needed my friend right next to me. Both Mom and Dad tried to comfort me, explaining that I should have been grateful that Amalia and I ever met. What if we'd never become friends? I knew that they were right. I knew that it was better to get to know each other so well than to never have met at all."

"Not long after, my mom had an idea: Why don't I write letters to Amalia every day? Not by email or text, but by hand as people used to write letters in the past. It would make me feel closer to her. I would be able to share all the things I used to tell her in person. Mom was right. It helped me a lot to overcome the sadness and the loneliness. Just describing my day, I understood that distance couldn't break a friendship. Distance could even make it stronger. Of course, I still wanted to see Amalia. But this way my days without her became brighter."

Even though we're a thousand miles apart, we'll still be best friends forever!

"I also wrote to her about my dream that one day we would travel to see each other again. And you know what? Our parents surprised us! Amalia's mom traveled to Dubai and brought her to visit us at our new home—without telling her that she would see me. My parents knew that they were coming and didn't say anything to me, either. So my mom told me that her friend was going to visit us, and when the bell rang, she told me to open the door. There was Amalia! Can you imagine our reaction? We were speechless! OMG! It was the best surprise ever!"

"Best of all, Amalia arrived just in time to see my first big performance. At the end, she presented me with a pink stuffed unicorn. I love unicorns, and I love my friend!"

"That time around, when she left Dubai, I didn't cry. I knew we would meet again. On my birthday Amalia sent me a slideshow of our photos and videos. On her birthday I sent drawings of our best moments together. We always love to laugh about how we first met. It was in the park across from school one day. Our moms had an immediate connection, but not Amalia and me. After only a few minutes of trying to play, we got into a fight. We didn't even want to talk to each other. But our moms solved everything with a Barni treat—a sponge cake bear with chocolate inside, which we both loved. And that's how our endless friendship started. Later we inaugurated Barni as a symbol of our friendship."

FUN FACT!
People often think that Michelle and Amalia are twins. Can you tell who is who?

"Being apart from Amalia taught me to value those precious moments together. Now I have a big dream to invite all my friends and cousins to a big performance. I will buy tickets for them and their parents, but I'll ask their parents not to tell them anything. Surprise!"
—DJM

It's so nice that Michelle got to see her friend again. Those who have actually lived in the UAE or other megapolises know how often people come and go from there. You have to say goodbye to so many friends. But it's the special ones who seem to stay in your life, especially if you work hard to keep in touch.

"The fact that Amalia arrived just in time to see me performing is just amazing, because music is so important to me. It's the friend that never leaves. Whatever I do and wherever I go, music is always with me. If I'm not home, I take my earbuds with me. If I am without earbuds, it's still in my heart and my soul. I can't live without it!"

It helps to have such great parents, too. Michelle agrees.

"Everybody knows that I am 'Daddy's girl,' and that's true. But there are certain things that I share with Mom only. Whenever I have some difficulties and I tell her that I want to talk, she turns into my friend, forgetting about being my mom. She is always ready to listen and give advice if I ask for it, then we discuss the possible solutions and pick the one that fits me. I think the best way to deal with life's hardships is to find somebody you trust—who can listen, understand you, and give the best advice. And for me, that's my mom."

And how does she end her day?

Usually with her parents, in front of the TV, watching some family movie or an educational show. They lie on the sofa, hugging each other under a cozy blanket. And then Michelle pretends that she falls asleep at the end so that her dad takes her to her bed, holding her in his arms.

Michelle adds, **"But *shhh*, never tell him—it's a secret."**

Don't worry, Michelle—your secret is safe with us!

THE LOCKDOWN

Time to pass the mic to Mom again! Let's talk about COVID-19 and how the lockdown affected home life and the whole family.

"Lockdown taught us all a lot: How to support each other, how to value all those precious moments we have together—as Michelle just mentioned—how to appreciate simple things and cherish life. It reminded us that the most important things in life are those we take for granted. Who could imagine that it would be such a wondrous relief just to walk outside your door and breathe without a mask? All the small worries disappeared at once, and our number one priority became clear: if we are safe and healthy, we can find true happiness.

"That said, at first it was difficult. These aren't just words; it was all real and happening in real life. It was especially hard for the kids. It's essential for them to take their energy outside, and do all those physical activities. And they need to communicate with each other. Luckily, there are phones and texts and social media for that. With the lockdown and COVID, we recognized the importance of the internet. One of the silver linings was that livestream DJ sessions started trending on Facebook and Instagram. We spent hours together watching D-Nice, Bob Sinclar, and other DJs. So we decided to start to go live ourselves with scratching, DJ sets, and Q & A sessions. The music and positive vibes were exactly what people needed."

D-Nice

Bob Sinclar

"It was a miraculous opportunity. Like never before, you could play for the whole world. People from a hundred different countries could watch you from the comfort of their homes! As a result, we spent more and more of our spare time livestreaming or filming videos of new routines. People kept telling us that we brightened their lives, put smiles on their faces, made their days . . . and they sent us videos, dancing to our music at home. Some even started their days with us. Their energy became our own, bringing a new wave of creativity and productivity."

Sounds like a feedback loop of awesomeness. There was no negativity, no hating. What a testament to the power of music—and one family's talent—they were able to turn a global pandemic into a healing moment.

Michelle really threw herself into DJing and music. She subscribed to the SUPER HERO DJs online school and started to learn the best worldwide routines. Right at the beginning of the pandemic, the Rasuls posted Michelle's video of the Stevie Wonder "Superstition" routine, which she learned from DJ Ride's lesson. It went viral. There were more than one million views on Michelle's page and more than ten million views on other pages, thanks to reposting. You can imagine how many messages and comments they received and still continue to receive.

Check out this amazing artwork made by the SUPER HERO DJs team

A NOTE OF GRATITUDE

"We are so grateful to each and every person who has ever supported us and been in touch with us. It's *you* who made Michelle famous. Without you nothing would happen. It's all thanks to your love and support, and we never could thank you enough for it! Music can transcend a terrible pandemic because music unites people. It feeds our souls and can change everything."

Michelle says it best: "Music is the best thing in the world! Music equals magic! It's my passion!"

"There is no greater joy than connecting with people on this planet. And we are so thankful that music connected us with you! There is a saying that the world will be saved by beauty. *Our* world—that of Michelle, Dad, and me—is always saved by music, love, and you!"

A FAMILY AFFAIR

Music is often a family affair. For as long as there have been musicians, parents like DJ Shock have passed on their passion and talent to children like DJ Michelle. And for as long as there have been pop stars, musical families like Michelle's have been lucky enough to share the limelight across generations. Think of Billy Ray Cyrus, who recorded his number one smash hit "Achy Breaky Heart" in 1992, the same year his daughter Miley, who went on to top the charts herself, was born. Or guitar virtuoso Eddie Van Halen, who in 2006 invited his fifteen-year-old son, Wolfgang, to join him and his brother in the family band . . . playing to millions of Van Halen fans across the world. Speaking of family bands, there are almost too many to name, from the Beach Boys and the Jackson Five to Echosmith and Haim. But the Rasuls might be unique in that the *entire* family is involved in the music business, and talent management comes with the package.

The Jackson Five

The Beach Boys

Michelle made it clear that she wanted to be a performer from a very early age. She was only three when she said, "I want to be on the stage." DJing wasn't the first thing that came to her parents' mind when she said that, but given their family, they knew that it had to be something related to music.

That was when they were still in Azerbaijan, in the capital, Baku, where Michelle was born. They started to try different classes, gymnastics and dance for the little ones held at the early learning center. Michelle enjoyed dancing a lot more than gymnastics. She didn't like when the trainer stretched her! But she started doing splits quite fast. Her parents' goal was to give her a chance to try different ways of expressing herself so she'd find her favorite. Then she could develop her skills and discover her talents to make it to the stage. That was one of the reasons they moved from Baku to Dubai—to give Michelle the opportunity to choose from the many more activities available there.

Van Halen, including Wolfgang's Uncle Alex

Miley and Billy Ray Cyrus

There are a lot of similarities between Dubai and Baku. Both are on the water; Dubai is on the Persian Gulf, and Baku, the Caspian Sea. Port cities tend to be highly diverse and cosmopolitan, open to outside cultures. So it was easy for the whole family to adapt to a new place for living. Michelle's mom remembers when they first arrived at their new home.

"When we just moved to Dubai, we were lucky enough to find out about a casting call for an upcoming kids' musical, *Visit to a Fairytale*— what a great opportunity to make it to the stage. And even more exciting was that the show was based on one of our family's favorite old movies! Michelle passed an audition where teachers of performing arts, music, and dance classes checked her skills. Then she started to attend the rehearsals with other artistic kids, who are still her good friends to this day.

Michelle was three years old when she looked at her baby photo with the Oscar statue in her mouth, and said to her mom, "Wait until you see me on TV!" And her mom answered: "I believe in you! It's only a matter of time!"

"When they were all set and ready to perform on stage, they visited a recording studio to record a song for the musical. How excited little Michelle was to be there! She had memorized all the lyrics and was carefully hitting each note of the song. It was so emotional to watch her sing this song our whole family had ties to at the studio. And the best part of the whole musical experience was that the show took place on the Dubai City Walk stage—the same place where Michelle later gave her first big performance as a DJ."

Performing all day every day

She had so much discipline for someone so young.

"She is just so at home on the stage and is a natural performer. Ever since her parents can remember, from when she was very little, she practiced on an improvised home stage a lot . . . like, several times a day. She always insisted that her 'shows' end with thunderous applause. Usually, she asked them to give her the bouquet of artificial roses they had at home."

Born for the stage, definitely. Also, born to get flowers.

"Roses are her favorite. It brought me so much joy when Dad presented her with a bouquet of *real* roses after the actual performance of *Visit to a Fairytale*. Michelle said she'd always fantasized that one day she would perform on a real stage in front of a large audience and receive the most beautiful flowers from her dad. So it was the first of many dreams come true. It was just like the name of the musical! I was sad when it came to an end."

Why did it come to an end? Couldn't she have taken the path toward acting?

"She definitely wanted to continue acting in musicals. After a few months, Michelle auditioned for another kids' musical. But this time Michelle wasn't selected because they needed kids with professional acrobatic skills—kids who could do splits and flips and other moves."

102

Was she disappointed? Let's see what Michelle's mom has to say about Michelle's reaction.

"No, it just made her want to try gymnastics one more time! She tried both the stylistic rhythmic gymnastics as well as the more technical artistic gymnastics, but ultimately it became clear she was more interested in DJing and dancing—she would watch dance tutorials on YouTube and show us the new routines every day! So, eventually, Michelle's passion for DJing and her love of dancing naturally directed us to the dance classes she started and happily continued until the pandemic struck. By that time, she'd already started performing as a DJ on the big stages. She'd already branded herself DJ Michelle. And the rest is history . . ."

Bet we all think that Mom's not giving herself enough credit! It also sounds like a ton of work, especially the brand part. Let's have a Q & A with Mom herself and see what she thinks about all these.

Branding takes a certain kind of creativity and organization. It really is a full-time job, isn't it?

"It is! And my previous experience as a brand manager really helps. I used to be senior brand manager for Baku's largest perfumery company. I would build for the local market an image of a world-known perfumery and cosmetics brand from the start—generating ideas and implementing them, developing promotional and advertising strategies, using my communication and organizational skills, along with my creativity, to achieve the goal. When it became clear that Michelle was serious and passionate enough to become a world-famous DJ, I had a goal again, and the skills to assist her on the way to her big dream."

What advice would you offer aspiring Momagers?

"If you have a unique talent and want to share your passion with the whole world, the internet and social media platforms give you an amazing opportunity to accelerate the process. If you have dreams, ideas—and you act upon them—you can create one-of-a-kind content around it. Step by step, your consistency and willpower will start producing the results. A dream with no plan is just a fantasy."

And you made Michelle's dream come true, too.

"Our objective was to use all our expertise to support her and to help develop her talent. After posting some of Michelle's videos, it was obvious that people loved watching her. We understood that if only she could reach a wider audience, the whole world would see a little girl who DJs like a pro. They would love her and follow her journey.

"Michelle's dad's role in her growth is huge. And as a mom, I wanted to contribute to their efforts using my skills, too. In the beginning, I wasn't an expert on social media, but we knew that an online presence was necessary. Before moving to Dubai, I took photography classes; I was always interested in creative photography. I practiced by taking children's portraits, which ended up giving me additional skills for creating a social media presence for Michelle."

"Of course, making a dream come true takes time and discipline—sticking to goals and taking them seriously. We all began to treat Michelle's goal as our full-time job, a job that we love. Almost every day brings new activities and something to learn. Whenever Michelle learns new scratches or creates new routines and wordplays, instead of filming home videos for our library we post them on social media. We believe that above all, it should serve as an archive of her growing up. The more people who discover her passion and dedication, the bigger and bigger it gets.

"We are always there for Michelle, and it's not only about DJing. If she has a new interest, we do our best to give her the chance to at least try it. When we moved to Dubai, the first thing she asked Daddy to buy was a Rubik's Cube. She'd seen a video of a kid who solved it. She always gets inspired after watching other talented kids. But neither Dad nor I were any good. Since she wanted to solve it so badly I started to search for tutorials. When I found the clearest explanation, I taught Michelle. She was so happy! You should have seen her after she solved it for the first time. Such bliss and happiness."

"When anybody asks me how I could reach such a high level at such a young age, I show them this photo."
—DJM

First steps

Michelle has a collection of Rubik's Cubes and currently solves 3x3 under 30 seconds, trying to beat her personal best results.

FUN FACT!

DJ Michelle is in good company when it comes to an obsession with the Rubik's Cube. Living legend Grandmaster Flash—founder of Grandmaster Flash and the Furious Five, the first hip-hop act ever to be inducted into the Rock and Roll Hall of Fame—is also obsessed. He was even featured in a 2017 National Geographic documentary about the Rubik's Cube, where he proclaimed that its inventor must have been "the geekiest geek of all."

Tell us about Michelle's dad's role in the Momager world.

"The whole book is not enough to describe her dad's role. Their bond is so special and precious. He is her friend, her mentor, her best supporter—and as Michelle says, the greatest and funniest dad in the world. He's doing everything he can and even more. I think all parents are managers in some way. It's our job to help kids discover their interests, strengths, and talents, and to nurture them till they grow big. All in an effort to help our children better position themselves in life, so they can be successful at whatever they do. Most of all, we have to help them believe in themselves, no matter what."

And accomplishing that is no easy task.

"Parenting is not always easy. We learn and we progress together with our children. With kids like Michelle—who are independent, who have strong personalities, who know exactly what they want—sometimes it's better to be an observer. You watch them instead of giving advice on what is right and what is wrong; you stay out and you don't impose your own point of view. It's not easy. Allowing them to learn from their own experience . . . your brain always tells you to protect them from making mistakes. Your brain wants to shout: 'Do as I said, because I know better.' But if you listen to your heart, it says: 'Relax. Let her take the lead. She will figure it out; it's all for the best.'"

Ever since she was a baby, Michelle would ask: Why are there a lot of songs about moms and so few about dads? So now she wants to dedicate her best song to her dad. Isn't it sweet?

"Raising Michelle, we tried to teach her to be kind and attentive to everyone, to be honest and respectful, and moreover to love herself and be true to herself. She is so young. Like every kid, she loves breaking the rules and crossing the lines. If we notice something troubling in her behavior, or if we just want to cheer her up, we often wait until the day is over. We tell her a bedtime story, recreating the situation with other characters in the lead role, so that she can step back for a moment and see the things from an outside perspective. And Michelle always concludes, 'The moral of the story is . . .'"

Perfect segue to the next question. How do you cope with disappointments or regrets—both hers and yours?

"Everybody makes mistakes. It's a part of learning. It was important to us from the start to explain that even the best DJs in the world can make mistakes, and it's totally okay. The main thing is how you deal with them and how you recover—to pick up yourself, move past it, and continue. Even if it's a big mistake, you can turn it into a joke or act as if it was a part of the performance . . . Michelle is lucky enough that she has never faced big problems and mistakes onstage. Her scratching is mostly freestyle and improvisation. Sure, there can be missteps, but she never stops."

The show must go on.

"True, and it's not always about the mistakes *she* makes! There are things beyond your control. Differences in the height of a DJ table can make for awkward hand positions during scratching. Or the equipment can fail. For example, recently we had a live event, and right at the beginning—already a thousand viewers were watching—her rig stopped working. Her dad wasn't around to help. It was Michelle's job both to fix it and to hold on to the audience. And she did it with confidence and a smile on her face: 'Guys, I have a little technical problem here, but give me a minute and we will start our fantastic party together!'"

"If you are not ready to deal with the mistakes, you could end up running away from the stage or hiding behind your deck. Nope, I won't do that!"—DJM 🙂

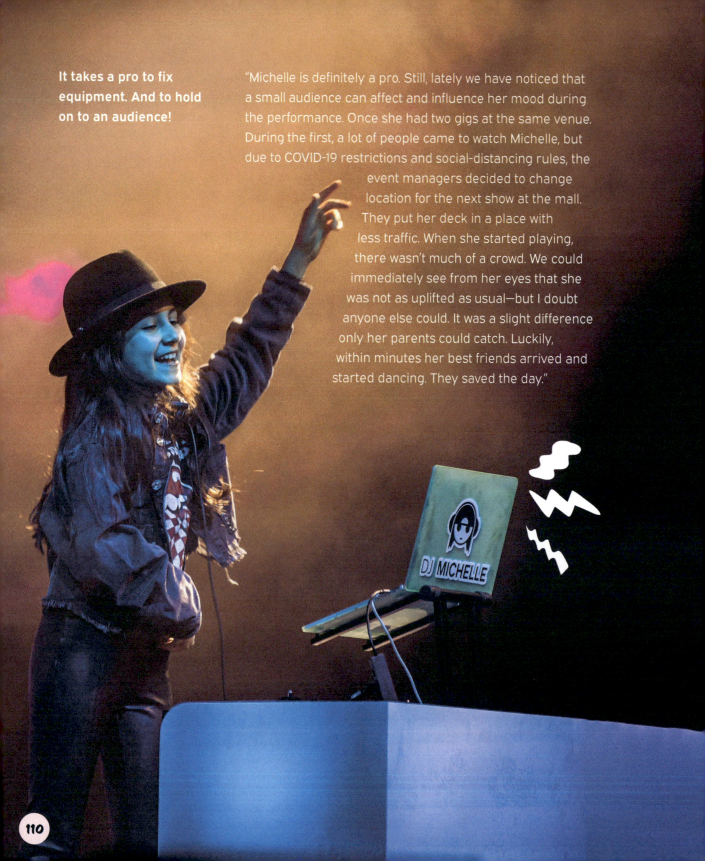

It takes a pro to fix equipment. And to hold on to an audience!

"Michelle is definitely a pro. Still, lately we have noticed that a small audience can affect and influence her mood during the performance. Once she had two gigs at the same venue. During the first, a lot of people came to watch Michelle, but due to COVID-19 restrictions and social-distancing rules, the event managers decided to change location for the next show at the mall. They put her deck in a place with less traffic. When she started playing, there wasn't much of a crowd. We could immediately see from her eyes that she was not as uplifted as usual—but I doubt anyone else could. It was a slight difference only her parents could catch. Luckily, within minutes her best friends arrived and started dancing. They saved the day."

Many artists experience that. Sometimes it is a humble reminder to reconnect with the basics of why we do what we do. But having friends show up—now that is a save! So as a mom and her manager, what words of advice did you give her after that second performance at the mall?

"I turned to her and said, 'Michelle, when you see only a few people around you, remember that even if you have a chance to encourage only one person with your art, it's already an accomplishment and success. Don't focus on the quantity, focus on the opportunity you have.'

"'But, Mom,' she told me, 'I am an artist. I need the response and the reaction of the crowd. I should feel their energy. The more people I see and the more feedback I have, the better!'

"Her dad nodded. 'I can relate to what she is talking about,' he said. But he's an artist and performer, too!"

Speaking of which, now seems like the perfect time to find out what happened at the 2021 DMC World DJ Championships!

"My heart belongs to the big stages! Nothing better than playing to thousands of people and seeing them vibing! I can imagine how it feels to stand on the biggest stages in the world. Another big dream? Yessss!"
—DJM 🙂

2021 DMC WORLD PORTABLIST CHAMPIONSHIPS

April 22–May 29

⭐ DJs show off their scratch skills on portable turntables!

⭐ This battle is for solo entry only.

⭐ The only gear permitted is an analog-only battery-powered portable turntable and vinyl records. Battery-powered analog mixer or fader is acceptable.

⭐ Elimination round: DJs submit a one-minute scratch video. Deadline is April 29th at 11:59 p.m. (EST). Judges will decide which DJs advance to the final round.

⭐ Final round: Finalists submit a two-minute scratch video. Deadline is May 16th at 11:59 p.m. (EST). Judges will determine the top winner, second, and third place.

⭐ Any battle submission cannot be more than four seconds past the required time limit or it will be automatically rejected.

⭐ Any video that is submitted after the deadline will not be accepted.

⭐ Good luck from the DMC team—we'll all be watching you!

It's April 30th. DJ Michelle is one of eighty-five contestants. Only the top ten advance to the finals. Did she have butterflies while she was waiting for the results? Michelle has a story to tell about that:

DAAAAAAD!!!!! YOU ARE IN THE FINALS!!!!!

"I was sure that at least one of us would advance to the finals, and I was so excited to hear that Dad made the top ten! When I heard that I placed fourteenth, I felt disappointment for only maybe a second . . . I would have loved to be there with him in the finals. But in a moment, I realized that coming in fourteenth out of eighty-five participants was a great achievement, especially since it was my first time competing in the DMC World DJ Championships. After that, I remember thinking, *Dad is in the top ten! Yay! I'm happy! Happy for us all! Even for those who didn't make it to the top fifteen! I'm happy for them because they tried!*"

She deserves a standing ovation just for being such a good sport.

It also meant she had time to assist her dad in preparing a new routine for the finals. She helped him choose the beat and sample! They joked around a lot and decided to make a funny video where her dad starts scratching, and Michelle sneaks up and speeds up the tempo.

"It was a blast. I think it's so important to have fun and appreciate the moment. Besides, if you do your best, put in all your heart, it means you are YOUR winner. In the end, I didn't care about a place that much. I just love competing and I love DJing! My parents taught me that it's never about the scores. You know, they don't even check my grades at school. (By the way, I have the best grades, though. 🙂) All that matters is dedication, effort, and attention.

"Whenever I do my best, I feel as if I have reached the highest peak of a mountain! And tomorrow I have a new mountain to climb and a new goal to reach. Again and again! Higher and higher! Better and better! And one day, I will surpass my dad and become a champion!"
—DJM 🙂

"I think that's also why I don't remember exactly which DJs I outperformed. There were about seventy. But I do remember some of the DJs who outperformed *me*. Of course, I totally agree with the decision of the judges about the winner, DJ Swordz. I would have given him the highest scores and the title of World Portablist Champion, too. The main thing for me is to look at the competitors without any jealousy and try to be objective. Tastes differ, but you can't close your eyes to professional skills; they are obvious and distinct."

That's a great takeaway.

The best takeaway for Michelle came from the legendary Tony Prince, the DMC organizer: "Every year we hope to see girls enter the DMC World DJ Championships challenge. There have been far too few in years gone by and so, from England, I gave DJ Michelle a standing ovation . . . Michelle is young and confident which is key to all things. At nine years of age she has a great image and could have a lot of fun with music, making a career and even outshining her dad, DJ Shock, in the future. Good luck, Michelle. Show the boys how it's done."

Sounds like she already has!

FAME

Even though he was born in Nicaragua, it's obvious to any true fan that DJ Craze (a.k.a. Arist Delgado) grew up in Miami. No matter what's spinning, you can hear the infectious influence of the Miami Bass Movement—known to fans as "booty music" since it always makes you shake your you-know-what—in his sound. On top of winning the DMC World DJ Championships three years straight (1999–2001), he has won over a dozen other DJ competitions around the globe. Like Michelle, he is also a producer. He founded the Cartel record label and cofounded Slow Roast Records with fellow DJ Kill the Noise. As for his style and where he sees it heading, he once said, "I can't honestly tell you . . . cause I'm constantly switching up my flow."

DJ Craze

Nowadays some might say that DJ Michelle is just as famous as DJ Craze. How has that changed her life? Does being famous affect her friendships? Michelle shares her feelings with us:

"When I first got into DJing, I didn't tell a lot of my friends because most kids that young don't really know what a DJ is! It would have been hard to explain to them what it was about. So most of the kids at my school didn't know about my passion. Though some of the teachers saw me DJing or got turned onto my videos—and every single one was so surprised. They couldn't believe it was me! They all asked me how it was even possible at my age.

"And when I started getting famous, I didn't want to tell kids about my DJing career and recognition, because it would sound like bragging. I want people to become friends with me for the same reason I want to become friends with *them*—not because they're famous, but because I like their personalities. I am a girl with a lot of hobbies, and I think all kids have different talents, and so I love making friends with kids that have interesting hobbies, too. But friendship has nothing to do with fame and if people try to get closer to you just because you are famous, that friendship won't last long. Usually, I only reveal my identity after someone has become a good friend."

119

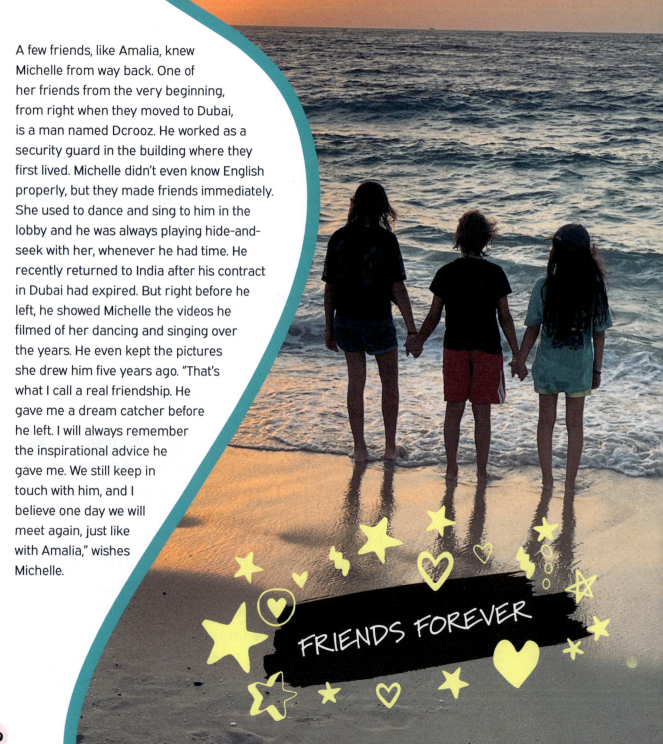

A few friends, like Amalia, knew Michelle from way back. One of her friends from the very beginning, from right when they moved to Dubai, is a man named Dcrooz. He worked as a security guard in the building where they first lived. Michelle didn't even know English properly, but they made friends immediately. She used to dance and sing to him in the lobby and he was always playing hide-and-seek with her, whenever he had time. He recently returned to India after his contract in Dubai had expired. But right before he left, he showed Michelle the videos he filmed of her dancing and singing over the years. He even kept the pictures she drew him five years ago. "That's what I call a real friendship. He gave me a dream catcher before he left. I will always remember the inspirational advice he gave me. We still keep in touch with him, and I believe one day we will meet again, just like with Amalia," wishes Michelle.

> Here's Dcrooz's message to Michelle

> Miss you Mimi! We met 5 years before! Always remember that time! You are my best friend! You gave lots of happiness to me. Danced for me, I still have that videos. And I still have your Christmas painting. I remember everything, and our last meet, and your gift. Your friend Dcrooz ❤️

Then there's the dog park. Michelle made friends with all of the dogs—plus their owners and trainers and also kids who came there for a walk—and no one knew about her career. She didn't tell anyone. Then one of her friends, Jada, the owner of a dog named Bunnie, discovered her Instagram page and sent her profile to the dog-owners group in WhatsApp. The message said something like: "You all know little Michelle as a sweet, kind girl and a dog lover, but I bet you didn't know she is that cool." They all were astonished to learn they'd been friends with the youngest girl DJ in the world the whole time!

MEET PABLO! ENGLISH BULLDOG, BORN July 18, 2021! By the time you see this, he is already a big boy!

"I think dog owners are the kindest people. They know everything about friendship and loyalty. I love all of them! Aaaand, I'm so happy to say that now I have a puppy too!!! His name is Pablo, and he is the best puppy ever! I'm telling you, dreams do come true!!!"
—DJM 🙂

Here's what Jada messaged to Michelle when she heard about her DMC story:

 jada_mayo So excited for you! This is amazing and couldn't happen to a more deserving human being! I'm so happy we met you, Bunnie misses you! You were always a bright light and now you're gonna shine like the star you are 🤩

"Recently I made two new friends from Germany, Nikaia and Emine. We were staying in the same hotel, and they found out everything from social media before I decided to tell them. We are best friends now! The good thing is they love music, too. It is so funny how we are alike in many ways. We have an extreme dream about creating a rock band. They have come to almost all the gigs I've ever had, since they know my secret. Our friendship is so exciting. We spend the holidays and weekends together and always find something interesting to do. They helped me to improve my swimming skills. They were also the reason I got interested in German. I love this language! And our friendship is forever!"

"You always make us smile, especially on that one live session on TikTok when we almost crashed the show by texting you things only we could know and you replied live. That was really amusing. But this is only one story of many."
—Nikaia & Emi

If the three friends did form a rock band, they would be in excellent company. Bands born in childhood friendships include the Beastie Boys, the Red Hot Chili Peppers, the Strokes, and the Black Keys. John Lennon was only sixteen when he met fourteen-year-old Paul McCartney . . . their band, the Quarrymen, eventually became the Beatles.

Ashanti

Soulja Boy

Kevin Lyttle

"What an honor to meet Till Lindemann himself—the frontman of the legendary Rammstein band—and to play an openning set for his concert on Dubai's biggest stage: the Coca-Cola Arena!" —DJM 🙂

One of her most special friends is Dany Neville, an award-winning DJ and producer from the UAE, who has performed in entertainment capitals around the world. He was the voice of the first urban radio program in the UAE. Back in the day, he was one of the youngest on-air personalities in the region, and now he is a star on Virgin Radio! And as if that wasn't enough, Dany is also a professional extreme sports athlete who has competed in some of the world's most prestigious competitions. "How proud I am to say that he is among a few favorite DJs who not only impresses me with his music knowledge and accomplishments but is also my friend!"

> **HERE IS HOW DANY NEVILLE DESCRIBES MICHELLE:**
>
> To me Michelle is a special soul.
>
> It's like I instantly connected with 10 year old Dany.
>
> Her artistic greatness within is so pure and innocent.
>
> In her mind she understands and feels home being a creative.
>
> It is her way of life and communication and I am humbled and honored to be a small part of it ❤️

"Music unites! It knows no boundaries and speaks all languages. Some friends I've never met in person, but we know each other from social media. I think it's really wonderful to have friends from different corners of the world and I hope one day we can meet and give each other a big hug. But music makes dreams come true! I'd always wanted to meet Wyclef Jean, who told me that I was his youngest carnival fan. (He also told me that he is a much bigger fan of me than I am of him! Noooo way!) Then it happened: During Global Citizen Forum 2022 in Ras Al Khaimah, we shared the stage. I love you, Uncle Wyclef, and hope to see you again very soon!"

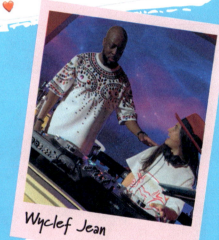

Wyclef Jean

"Of course, for some people I will always be that energetic girl who wears fun clothes, always has earbuds in, and carries a slingshot in her pocket. But for my closest friends, I can be those things as well as a world-famous DJ, and I love that!"
—DJM 😊

Let's go back over to Mom to discuss Michelle's fame.

Saida, when did the press first start reaching out about Michelle?

"In 2018, Saif Abdulla—radio and podcast host, MC, and author—contacted us for the interview with Michelle at Pearl FM UAE, a radio station for children and families. Michelle was six and had just started to gain popularity. It was so unexpected to receive an invitation for an interview, which made it so emotional and memorable. Saif was the first media personality who noticed her talent and believed in her bright future. He reaches and uplifts all the kids of the region, so we feel particularly blessed that he always comments on Michelle's achievements, encouraging her with his kind and motivational words."

Michelle is incredible, talented and inspirational. She works really hard and she always smiles and spreads happy energy around the UAE. Following your parents steps is an absolute blessing. You are a star and remember to always shine bright..
Saif Abdulla

"Two months after the first interview, Michelle was invited to another radio station—Hit 96.7 FM, part of the Arabian Radio Network. At the same time, Michelle's first printed interview appeared in *Gulf News*, and her story was posted on CNN Arabic's official site."

"After Michelle was chosen to become a Numark Brand Ambassador (and the youngest Numark Ambassador ever) *DJane Mag Brasil*—a DJ magazine for women—contacted us for an interview. Michelle has a lot of followers from Brazil. She dreams about meeting them on a world tour!

"Soon after that, the interviews became nonstop . . . *Khaleej Times* interviewed her . . . then came a TV interview for Sony TV . . . then Channel 12 Israel, featuring Michelle and Aviel Brant, who was the first Israeli DJ to travel to the UAE after the borders were opened. There was also an interview on *The Magic Phil Show*, the UAE's favorite kids' magician and radio host, and a Pulse 95 Radio interview with the one and only Ana Schofield and Big Hass, who had witnessed Michelle's career growth from the very beginning."

MICHELLE; MEET 7-YEAR-OLD DJANE NAMED AMBASSADOR FOR THE NUMARK

Exclusive interview with little Michelle from Dubai who is already an Instagram phenomenon. Her innocent charisma, technique and performances catch the eye of many DJs and celebrities around the world.

1magicphil
DJ Michelle brings so much magic to the decks and is an inspiration to all youngsters xx

big_hass
Groundbreaking and an inspiration to young and upcoming Djs. Age is just a #

127

So many of these appearances sound special and deeply personal. It's clear you take nothing for granted.

"Very true. At the end of 2020, Nickelodeon chose Michelle as one of eight kids to represent the 'International Extraordinary Me' campaign. A short film is broadcasting on Nickelodeon channels around the world, featuring each of the eight's unique stories. Today a lot of kids still call Michelle 'the girl from Nickelodeon.' But naturally, the biggest media exposure started right after Michelle entered the DMC World Portablist Championships."

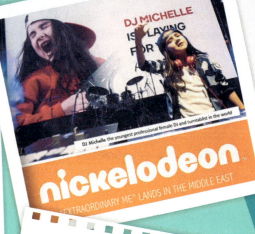

How did that change things?

"There was a time when Michelle had several interviews a day. When Associated Press contacted us to film an interview about Michelle's scratching skills, DJ career, and everyday life, we didn't expect it to fly around the world so fast. If you Google search 'DJ Michelle at DMC Championships,' you will see how many channels shared the interview, including CNN Radio, *New York Post*, NowThis News, Yahoo! News, Arab News, Gulf Today, Xeber Xetti (Azerbaijan News), *Khaleej Times*, the *Seattle Times* . . . just to name a few."

"We could hardly manage to check all the direct messages from social media. One of the most special and meaningful interview requests came from the If I Could series in *Nargis*—the most famous magazine in Azerbaijan, our motherland."

"It would also be fair to mention how we were thrilled when Mihaela Noroc—a world-famous Romanian photographer who has been featured by *Forbes*, CNN, the BBC, and *O, The Oprah Magazine*—came to Dubai to photograph Michelle. Mihaela Noroc made a name for herself by traveling the world, taking pictures of amazing women, and listening to their stories. Now she is doing the same with a select group of extraordinary little girls, spread all around the globe, for an upcoming book, *The Little Atlas of Beauty*. What a great honor to be a part of this incredible project!"

Backstage photo from Mihaela's photoshoot

Tell us a little bit about the interview process. Does it ever become exhausting or tedious?

"No, never. Some of the interviews are via Zoom—France's BFMTV, Dubai Eye 103.8 FM, *Kidsweek* newspaper from the Netherlands . . .

"Recently, Michelle was interviewed by Tessy Antony de Nassau—the former princess of Luxembourg—who is now a social entrepreneur, businesswoman, philanthropist, UNAIDS Ambassador (Global Advocate for Young Women and Adolescent Girls), public speaker, activist . . . and most importantly, an amazing person and mother. Michelle was thrilled to be chosen as a guest for her podcast, *Tessy Antony de Nassau's Zoom O'Clock*, especially after Tessy told us that she'd hosted many global leaders and celebrities but never a young girl with such a great passion for music. We were so happy and honored to meet her.

"Sometimes she is invited to the studios, like Panorama FM in Dubai . . . or filmed at home, like when a German TV team traveled to Dubai just for Michelle. The interviewers almost always ask the same questions, but all of them have a unique flavor and approach. So every interview is different, and they all stand out from one another. Once Michelle was even interviewed by a boy her age, Eden, for KEA Kids News. They had so much fun doing it! Often during interviews, we talk about Michelle's relationship with her dad. For example, DubaiLAD—a well-known media platform in the UAE—filmed a short story about Michelle and her dad. They showed that there is no age and no gender limit when it comes to achieving your dreams."

What a message about age and gender. Girl Power! It's hard to think of a better example. Would you say the 2021 DMC World DJ Championships was really the turning point for Michelle? Is that when she went from Dubai sensation to global phenomenon?

"Absolutely. I remember how honored and surprised we were when the people from NPR's *Morning Edition* reached out when she placed fourteenth. NPR needs no introduction! And we were so excited to listen to the interview after it went live—to hear the host, Lulu Garcia-Navarro, exclaim to millions of listeners, 'One of the world's best DJs is only nine years old!' I kept thinking, *This is our daughter. Our Michelle. Wow. Just Wow.* Never did we dream that it all would turn into this!

"This book wouldn't have happened if it weren't for that interview, either. One of those millions of listeners was an editor from Blackstone Publishing!"

SMASHED IT!

Now, let's hear again from the star herself and learn about the most rewarding experience she's had so far.

"**It might have been my performance at Sample Music Festival. I was seven, and it was the first time I had to show off my scratching skills to a live audience of adult DJs and musicians. That extra responsibility made me feel great, and I was so proud of myself at the end. It's sort of funny, though: now I can see how simple my scratches were back then. But I also see that I was brave, and that stayed with me.**"

"The biggest reward for me is the joy of doing what I love. that's when I'm happiest!" —DJM 🙂

"In 2019, I won first place at the Rags-to-Riches DJ competition, sponsored by American Rag Cie and the Dubai Shopping Festival. Contestants had to play ten-minute sets, any genre, judged equally by track selection, musicality, technical skills, overall impact, and stage presence. There were seven participants including me. The other six were adult men! So it was so cool and unexpected when I took first place. The judges told me that they had seen me scratching but didn't know that I had a nice mixing technique! As a winner, I also got the chance to spin monthly at American Rag Cie.

By just eight years old, Michelle became not only the youngest contestant but a finalist at the Goldie Awards! INCREDIBLE!!!

"I also feel fortunate that so many big celebrities have supported me. Heroes of mine, stars like Missy Elliott, Wyclef Jean, Chris Brown, Pharrell, Timbaland, J Balvin, the Black Eyed Peas, La Toya Jackson, DJ Premier, Claptone, DJ Khaled, DJ Snake, Bob Sinclar, B-Real, Too $hort, Mr Eazi, Afro B, Gashi, Fatboy Slim, Alicia Keys—all of them reposted or reacted to my videos. Every time I see their comments my heart beats so strong that I think you can hear it on the other side of the world. I can't help but scream and jump on the bed! To be noticed by the legends is the biggest reward for me. I am so motivated after I see encouraging comments or fire emojis from artists I love! I wish I could meet them all and ask them to sign vinyl for my collection one day."

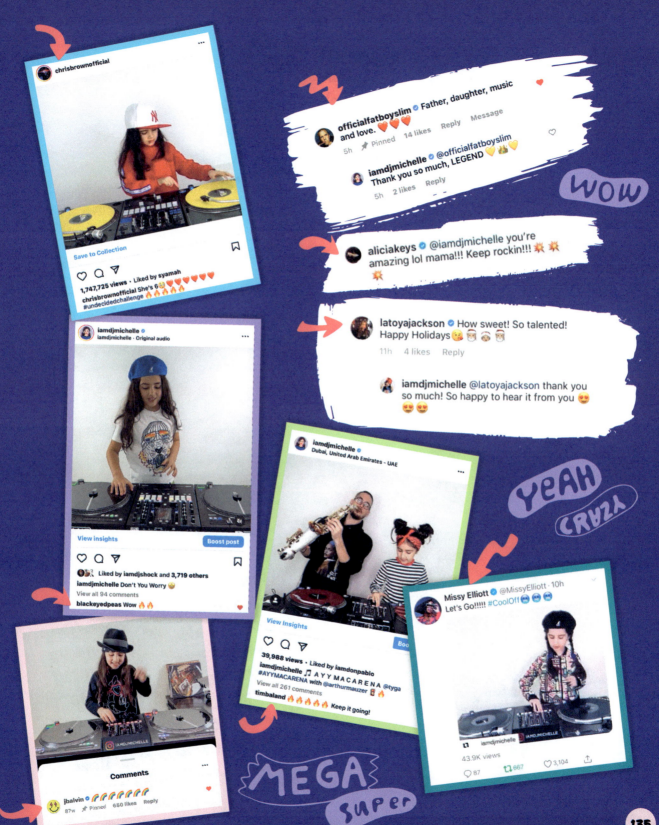

"On top of being a Global RANE Artist, I am also a Nike Ambassador. It is such an honor to represent these big brands and to be a part of the teams!" —DJM 🙂

wow

Cool!

"I love that Nike is focused on the idea of play as a foundation of sport for kids. If you come up with a new dance, if you play tag with friends—to the Nike team it's a sport too, and you are an athlete, because you don't do sports, you *play* sports! How cool is that?" —DJM 🙂

MICHELLE IS BAGGING MULTIPLE ENDORSEMENTS AND WORKING WITH FASHION BRANDS. SHE HAS HAD SO MANY COOL LOOKS OVER THE YEARS!

Michelle isn't afraid to show her FASHIONABLE side!

More Girl Power! Those are such huge successes. Are you all curious to know if DJ Michelle ever had a surprising experience that wasn't exactly what she expected?

"Life isn't only about *yes*. Sometimes you grow more when you hear *no*. If you choose to compete, you have to be ready to fail. My parents explained to me that everything depends on my perception. If you take third place in the competition, you could accept it as winning—as long as you continue doing your best to achieve better results and treat the previous experience as motivation to improve your skills. If you feel you lost, you risk the opposite, to give up and stop all your efforts."

"Here's a perfect example. In 2020, I was invited to participate in the fifteenth season of *La France a un incroyable talent*—the French version of *America's Got Talent*—but because of the pandemic we couldn't travel and had to decline the offer. It was so disappointing, but the next year we received the invitation again and were able to accept. We traveled to Paris, and I even memorized enough French to introduce myself on stage and perform a two-minute routine that included wordplay, scratching, and beat juggling.

"Paris was amazing. I felt the connection with this beautiful city right from the first minute . . . maybe because I have a French name? Everything felt perfect. It was organized, the team was super friendly, and Bob Sinclar even recorded an encouraging message just for me! If you ask me who my favorite DJs are besides those who scratch, Bob Sinclar would be one of the first on the list. And it was FANTABULASTIC to receive a message from him!"

"Since I am a scratch DJ, I naturally assumed that they had invited me on the show to see scratching. Performance day started early. We were required to be in the building at nine a.m. for the rehearsals and behind-the-scenes filming. My performance didn't start until after three p.m., and by that time we were all so tired. Mom and Dad started worrying about how difficult it would be for me to summon my energy and give the kind of performance I always gave. But I did! My parents were on set, and they saw how I completely gave myself over to my passion and the moment. I thought the judges would see it, too, and send me to the semifinals. Instead, I got two votes *yes* and two votes *no*. One of them said that she would have loved to hear less scratching and more dance music. I was out of the competition and wouldn't be advancing. I was so shocked that I couldn't find anything to say. After a humble, '*Merci beaucoup*,' I left the stage."

"Hearing *no* was very unexpected, especially since I got a standing ovation at the start of the performance. Some of the judges stood up and danced. One even bounced over and danced beside me! Running offstage, I started to cry. Dad and Mom thought I was upset because I hadn't advanced to the semifinals. They were wrong. The tears came because I was *angry* at the judges for not understanding real DJing! As it turned out, we later learned the judges expected me to do simple and uncomplicated things. They weren't into DJing. For people who are not into DJing, our skills can seem too technical and difficult to understand."

It took time for Michelle to accept what happened. After nerves settled, her mom and dad helped her realize that it was a great lesson.

"Now I am grateful for what I learned! Not all people will love or even understand your skills. Nobody is an expert in everything. All of the greats suffered loss and rejection along the way. It's part of the journey."

Michelle loves the saying,
"Sometimes you win, sometimes you learn."

WHAT NEXT?

DJ Michelle is taking lessons in music production and has started creating her own music. She dreams of creating worldwide hits! She also resumed finger-drumming lessons. At the beginning of her DJ career, she used to do it while her dad was scratching. But then as she threw herself more into DJing she forgot about it. Since she's decided to give it a try again, she realized she likes it! As with any other skill, it takes time and effort to advance. Let's see how far.

"I also started to train my left hand in scratching. My goal is to reach the same level as I reached with my right hand. It's not easy at all, and I feel like a beginner all over again. But if I can master difficult scratches with my left hand and start scratching equally well with both hands, I will be one of the very few DJs who can do it! Shoutout to DJ Craze!"

"Finger drumming" means using your fingers as drumsticks—in rhythm and in real time, triggering samples and making beats.

"Mastering the bass guitar and drums is also one of my biggest dreams. I want to play like a pro. I hope one day to call myself a professional drummer and bass player. So once I become DMC World Champion—I believe it will happen!—I see myself performing in Tomorrowland, traveling the world with my DJ sets, playing drums and bass in a rock band . . . Not much different than today! When I dream that all my friends and family will attend my big concerts in different corners of the world, I also dream that I meet them backstage right afterward and spend a great time together exploring whatever country we're in. I see myself enjoying life, spreading love and happiness through my music."

And writing. Michelle also wants to become an author and write fantastic books for kids that help them to achieve their dreams and desires.

Well, we're happy to report, Michelle, that that dream has already come true. You *are* an author!

"Oh, right! I am. So what else? I also want to open a music school where kids like me can study the regular subjects such as language arts, math, and science together with DJing, music theory, solfeggio, history of music, and instrumental performance. And I also want to create a World DJ Kids competition—do you think it's a nice idea? Because I do. And when I am my parents' age, I want to continue doing what I love. And when I have kids, if they are as crazy about music and DJing as I am, I will start to teach them young—as my parents taught me. Who knows? Maybe they will start DJing even earlier than I did. That would be fun!"

FUTURE

One day, Michelle wants to compete in Rubik's Cube championships and set the new record!

"It's never too early and never too late to start following your dreams!" —DJM

Michelle is also known for spreading positivity and inspirational messages to her fans. Here is what she would advise not only aspiring artists and musicians, but all who want to succeed:

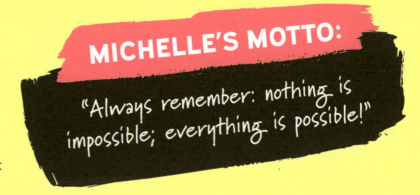

MICHELLE'S MOTTO:

"Always remember: nothing is impossible; everything is possible!"

"My message always remains the same—to all the kids and grownups out there, no matter if they are musicians or not: passion has no age and no gender. Follow your heart, find your obsession, do everything to master and extend your knowledge and talent. Find yourself a mentor and the person who lifts you up. Try to organize yourself and be consistent, even if the progress comes slow—the things that look hard get easier. Give it time and enjoy every little step toward your goal. No matter who you want to be, always believe in yourself, never give up, and continue practicing and doing your best. Above all, have fun, be happy with what you do, and always remember: nothing is impossible; everything is possible!"

To the parents of aspiring artists or musicians, Michelle's mom says:

"Michelle's dad and I believe that *all* kids are gifted. You just need to discover where their talents lie. We parents can only support them, believe in them, and help them to find and use the right instruments to succeed. Cultivating their early interests and strengths, listening and talking to them, guiding them, and nurturing their individuality and self-confidence . . . it all helps a lot. We prefer to focus more on a child's excitement rather than results. Our hope, always, is that Michelle inspires as many kids and their parents as possible.

145

Planting a love of reading is always helpful. Later, we can help steer them toward books with characters who share their traits or circumstances or who motivate them. If your child is artistic in any way, finding the right educational tools and equipment is one of the best ways to develop their potential. And we are not talking about expensive stuff here—we were always against the fancy toys for kids, and Michelle's first DJ controller wasn't expensive at all. Pricey stuff doesn't have to do with success. You don't need the latest upgraded equipment—you just need to start. Photographers always say, 'It's not the camera, it's the photographer!' What would the camera be in the hands of an impassionate photographer, right? So don't focus on the equipment and high-end gear too much. Just give your kids all you can give at the moment, one step at a time. There is no precise recipe for parents. Sometimes just your presence or a simple hug can work wonders. I remember hearing about a dad who tried to break-dance because his son was interested in learning how, just to be a good example. That's successful parenting in my book!"

"This reminds me of the lyrics Michelle and I rewrote for John Lennon's anthem song to support the UNICEF-led #IMAGINE initiative:

Imagine every kid on the planet is an angel, who landed,
Allow them to be happy, be kind, be the best Mom and Daddy!
Spoil them, hug them, and always say that you love them!
Protect them, respect them, accept them as they are,
And don't try to change them!
Imagine every kid on this planet has a unique talent!
Just believe it, support them, and help them to find it!
You may say I'm a dreamer, but I'm not the only one!
I hope someday you'll join us, and let children shine their light!"

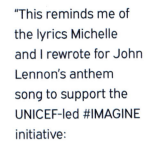

147

DUBAI EXPO 2020
EPILOGUE BY MICHELLE

In 2021, the UAE hosted Dubai Expo—a giant world exhibition with individual pavilions that feature 192 countries around the globe—and Michelle was invited to perform! Here's what she has to say about that experience.

To get there, we met with the participants at a hotel where the buses were waiting to transfer us to the Millennium Amphitheatre. I felt like a big star on a world tour, moving from bus to bus filled with skaters and BMXers, B-boys and B-girls, MCs and beatboxers, rappers and street artists—and all from different countries! OMG!

Michelle

As soon as we arrived at Al Forsan Park, we were given instructions and the show schedule, and then came what has become my favorite part: sound check. It's still about the butterflies in my stomach like it was that first time, but now I also love standing on the stage, looking down on the empty chairs. And there were *a lot* of them. Soon they would be filled. I couldn't wait to spread the good vibes!

After the sound check, we had a break, and my parents bought me a special Expo "passport" which has a unique number and watermark images on each page. You can even include your photo, too! So then when I visited the pavilions of different countries, I got their stamp on my passport! Mini world tour! So cool!

While I waited to take the stage, I loved watching all the performers. What impressed me the most were the B-boys with disabilities. But here in the UAE, we don't say "people with disabilities," we say "people of determination." And now I know exactly what that means. I've never seen more determined people in my life. They are my heroes, the ones who deserve to be on the covers of the magazines, the subjects of books and documentaries. They show us that nothing is impossible. I can only imagine how much work and effort they put in to learning a single trick.

All the amazing performers were mostly invited from different countries to participate in the show. I got to watch skaters during their rehearsal and then see them on the stage. I tried to memorize their tricks, because guess what I was planning to do the next morning? Right! Skating!

#READYTOROCK

That night, when it was my turn to perform, I heard the MC say my name, and the crowd roared. *It's time!* I thought, and that old excinervousness came rushing back. But once I was up there, I felt right at home. I started with my routines on the turntables, then Dad joined me for our B2B set. What a night! I enjoyed every second. We played funk, old-school hip-hop, and B-boys tunes. When we came offstage, the MC and one of the organizers told me, "You killed it."

You know what I replied? "I know." 😊

And he said, "You *should* know, because you did. I love your confidence. You were probably the best part of the whole show!"

Can you dig it?

FANTABULASTIC!

Michelle! ☺